A Catholic Guide to the Mature Years

Msgr. Charles Fahey & Edward Wakin

Our Sunday Visitor, Inc.
Huntington, Indiana 46750

Library of Congress Catalog Card No.: 84-60747
ISBN: 0-87973-603-8

CONTENTS

PREFACE

Welcome to the Third Age of Your Life

AT AGE 47, the typical American is going full speed with job, family, career and community involvements.

Age 47 is a significant time to mark off on life's calendar for two demographic reasons:

At the turn of the century, the average American would have been dead at that age.

Today, not only is the average American alive and well at that age, so are his or her parents and a whole third of a lifetime lies ahead.

This book is about getting the most out of that *third age* of life. At that point, an individual is established in a way of life and at the threshold of new options, new choices and new opportunities. This book goes forward from that challenging threshold in order to examine life in the *third age*.

It is a third major period of life, following the *second age* of getting established in job, career and family. Further back there is the *first age* of growing up and getting an education.

For some men and women in the *third age*, change is thrust upon them by an empty nest, by marital separation, divorce or widowhood or by economic upheavals in job and career. For others, change is a matter of choice. It is a decision to move in new directions.

The vista of a fulfilling and challenging *third age* is unfolding for an increasingly higher proportion of Americans — the two out of five adults who are 50 or older. Yet very little has been done to chart the opportunities, challenges and choices facing them. That lifetime mapmaking can be done at any point in the *third age*, but the sooner the better. Rather than a surprise and a trauma, retirement should unfold as part of the process of moving through the *third age* of life.

Our basic message is simply this: Pay attention, explore your *third age*, plan, adjust and discover how you can get the most out of it in the spirit of Christian fulfillment.

‡ ‡ ‡

ONE

A New Outlook

THE OUTLOOK for mature Americans is a longer, healthier and more fulfilling life than ever before in the history of the nation or, for that matter, the world. Old attitudes, traditional viewpoints and long-standing assumptions face dramatic revisions. In short: we are facing a new outlook toward growing older.

This means new opportunities and greater challenges for the two out of five Americans who are 50 or older. For American society in general and the Catholic Church in particular, this also means greater challenges. New realities demand new responses.

However, mature Americans — as well as church and state — are only beginning to become aware of the new realities. Their adjustments are still in the formative stages. Personal and professional planning for change is still handicapped by limited awareness; not enough people and institutions are doing something to benefit from the available opportunities. Changes are being registered as if they are distant rumblings felt by a seismograph when actually here and now they are remaking our lives and our society.

Age has lost its clarity. It no longer makes sense to divide Americans by age into simple categories, and it is ridiculous to use age as the basis for deciding how to live, where to work, what to do, and how to function in home, church, school and community situations.

Age is no longer the dictator it once was. What counts today is the overall life situation in which individual men and women find themselves. This has come about because of a true revolution in demographics: men and women are living longer, healthier and more active lives than ever before in the history of humankind.

For Americans in their late 40s, a whole third of a lifetime lies ahead as life expectancy climbs into the mid-70s. That remaining one-third of the life-span is a *third age*. The new demographic reality calls for a revised outlook on getting older and overthrows outmoded cliches on young and old, active and inactive, involved and uninvolved.

As Dr. Robert Butler, a leading authority on aging, has stated: "This is the first time in human history that the chance of living out the whole life cycle is better than otherwise."

When a lifetime is viewed in "three ages," then the notion of aging is revolutionized. Basically, the three ages divide as follows:

First age — Beginning at birth, the *first age* of life revolves around family and school. Parents are the central figures, followed by teachers and friends. Each individual is going through the process of growing up physically, emotionally, intellectually, psychologically and spiritually. Each is dependent, each struggling and straining toward independence. Each is reacting — to others, situations, demands, requirements and expectations. It is the age of getting ready for responsible adulthood by learning, by developing and by acquiring skills. It is the age of preparation.

Second age — Typically launched when an individual begins working full time in job and career, the *second age* is the time for establishing a place in society. The individual faces the demands of work and the task of paying his or her own way. Marriage and then child rearing open up new directions as they also set boundaries and impose responsibilities. Pressures and satisfactions arise from making a living, building a career and taking care of a family. Energies are directed toward specific goals: getting ahead, paying the bills, helping children to develop from one stage to the next, meeting the demands of participation in church and community. It is the age of undertaking roles, an age of application and clearly defined responsibilities.

Third age — When an individual is established and when the major demands of building a career and/or parenting are over, the *third age* dawns. The age of 50 is only a rule of thumb for marking off this age, because it is not a chronological category. It is a social, psychological, economic and religious reality. In the *third age* an individual has established a level of success and achievement, and, if a parent, the children are grown and on their own. It is the age of new choices.

With choice come the opportunities to aim for new horizons and for greater fulfillment. In the *third age*, there are fewer dictates and outside restraints, because the doubts and uncertainties about getting ahead no longer are in the foreground and because the demanding task of parenting is typically replaced by the relaxed role of grandparent.

As with all categories, the *third age* is a generalization. Many men and women have some, but not all the characteristics of the *third age*. They may reach a career plateau, but still have children in college or graduate and professional schools. That would delay the arrival of the *third age* situation, while others in their mid-40s have grown-up children who are on their own. Regardless, the concept of a *third age* provides a clearer and surer way of facing the present and planning for the future. *This approach benefits men and women approaching the third age and those in any part of the third age.*

A focus on the *third age* is more meaningful, more fulfilling and more realistic than a focus on retirement. The *third age* is that time of life when we begin to look differently at time and money and their place in our lives. This change in outlook occurs long before retirement. It arrives on entering the *third age* of different demands, different responsibilities, different opportunities.

In order to draw a statistical portrait, age 50 is a convenient landmark provided by U.S. Census data. The following emerges:

- About 40 percent of over-49s are still working.
- Among the 15 percent who are retired and active, half are 65 to 75, almost one-third over 75.
- Some 20 percent are full-time homemakers. The largest proportion of these women is married — 70 percent. One-fourth is widowed.

Over-50 Americans are growing in numbers at a rate of twice that of the American population and have $500 billion in spending power. (There is another side to this economic picture with regard to the minority — 17 percent — of the over-50 Americans who are economically disadvantaged. They represent a serious challenge to government policy. This 17 percent and another six percent listed as "other" by the U.S. Bureau of the Census complete the breakdown of the over-50 population in the Census data.)

Madison Avenue is finally discovering the economic importance of the *third age* as are all the media. As one advertising executive, Rena Bartos, reported in the *Harvard Business Review*: "The over-49 market seems to be in a discovery stage analogous to the early 1970s when some marketers 'discovered' the working woman market.''

Media ''discovery'' of this reality was epitomized by a front-page headline in an issue of *USA TODAY:* OVER-65s WILL OUTNUMBER TEENS IN JULY. The article reported that for the first time in U.S. history there will be more people over 65 than teenagers. By the year 2020 those over 65 will outnumber teenagers two-to-one.

Meanwhile, medical progress and greater attention to personal health have overturned the myth that vitality and an active life depend on age. At a certain fixed age, men and women don't change from productive, involved, active individuals into bumps on a log. We forget that age 65 was chosen arbitrarily as a retirement age in 19th-century Prussia under Bismarck. It was chosen for reasons of administrative simplicity so that people who survived at that age would receive benefits they earned. By contrast, it is now truer than ever in history that you are only as old as you feel.

Medical progress has reduced the impact of chronic diseases and protected us from diseases that have plagued humankind throughout history. For example, if turn-of-the century mortality rates prevailed today, almost 400,000 Americans would die this year from tuberculosis; 300,000 from gastroenteritis; 80,000 from diphtheria, 55,000 from poliomyelitis. Instead, the combined death toll of all four diseases is less than 10,000.

TIME magazine's description of U.S. Representative Claude Pepper paid tribute to the vitality that can last a lifetime with the aid of medical science: Congressman Pepper ''watches the world through trifocals. He wears a pacemaker in his chest to quicken his heartbeat when it slows. One of his heart valves is synthetic; it replaced the natural one that developed a calcium deposit. He is nearly deaf without his hearing aids. . . . He is 82 years old. . . . [He] is like a vintage automobile with new parts: he gets better and more powerful with age.''

Visit, for a moment, the Citizens' State Bank in Dalhart, Texas, at 10 o'clock on a weekday morning along with a reporter from *The Wall Street Journal.* He poured himself a cup of coffee and joined some men in a back room at the bank:

> The men, in their late 70s and early 80s, have been getting together for coffee every morning for more than 30 years to trade gossip about this small town's affairs. These days their conversations invariably will turn, at some point, to matters of health, either their own or someone else's. And if a visitor listens carefully, a rather remarkable fact will emerge: All the men have suffered illnesses that in years past would have left them bedridden or dead. Yet they have all been successfully treated, and while they aren't as spry as they used to be, they are still active in Dalhart's daily life.

Or switch to New York's Avery Fisher Hall on March 11, 1983 and the experience reported by *The New York Times* reviewer Donal Henahan: ''All those who were fortunate enough to be in Avery Fisher Hall last night will be able to tell incredulous listeners in years hence that they heard Andrés Segovia give a technically fluent, mesmerizing recital when he was a month past his 90th birthday.''

Pablo Picasso the painter, Frank Lloyd Wright the architect, and Bertrand Russell the philosopher all were productive and active past the age of 90. Ronald Reagan in the White House will always stand out in U.S. history as a forceful refutation of myths about aging. As Picasso once commented: "Age only matters when one is aging. Now that I have arrived at a great age, I might just as well be 20."

Famous examples of living longer and actively are only the tip of the iceberg. All over the country, men and women are demonstrating the same demographic reality. There are such examples as veterinarian Louis J. Camuti of Mount Vernon, New York, who until his death at 87 made house calls to treat cats; or Joseph Miceli, who was still cutting hair at age 80 for visiting dignitaries and just plain tourists at New York's Carlyle Hotel, or flying instructor Leo Leydecker of Buffalo, New York, who celebrated his 80th birthday by flying a Cessna over Western New York. Then there is TV commentator Dorothy Fuldheim, who appeared on Cleveland's home screen from the dawning of television. At the age of 89, she signed a new three-year contract.

Americans in the *third age* are active, involved, and independent. Of all Americans 50 and over, only one percent are ill or disabled. Among the elderly, only five percent are confined to their homes, only one percent bedridden. The outlook for the Catholic Church, for individuals and for the society as a whole is a *third age* full of life and living. What we are beginning to realize — and it cannot be repeated too often — is that there is a difference between longevity and age, between how long we have been doing something and how old we are. We can become stale and worn-out at any age; that depends on how long we have been doing the same thing in the same place for the same purposes.

Take the example of a pastor in a church. The tendency is to say, "Monsignor is no longer a good pastor because he is old." The real reason may be that he is no longer a good pastor just because he has been in the same parish for too long a time.

There is no disease of old age. There are diseases that occur more frequently in later years or they become more enervating, but there is no disease of old age.

Given the favorable medical report for the *third age*, the two major variables are time and money. Early in the *third age*, the supply of either or both is likely to increase. As children finish their education, parents are freed of the high cost of schooling, particularly if sons and daughters attend private colleges. When children grow up, the responsibilities of parenting disappear; even more so when children leave the family nest. At retirement, the amount of time increases, though not the amount of money.

More time and/or money mean more options, choices and alternatives. They call for decisions as the *third age* dawns, not at retirement time, since by then important changes have already taken place that mark a different life situation. Change can be viewed as a threat or as an opportunity. If an individual is aware of change and seeks out worthwhile choices, then change can be a friend.

On one hand, it is important to maintain continuity and to build on our past. On the other hand, it is necessary to identify turning points in life as the time to make choices. It is that way throughout life. Certain points, such as graduation from school, looking for a job, courtship and marriage, involve obvious choices. Upon entering the *third age*, choices may be masked and may be postponed. But no less necessary, sooner or later.

Because of new freedom, particularly when grown children are out of the house and on their own, *third age* people need to reassess the place where they live, the activities they pursue, even the job they hold. They need to look around and examine their friendships and their interests. Is it time to change, to move out in new directions?

In particular, it is a time to identify talents and interests that have long been dormant. Is it a desire to go back to school? To pursue a new hobby? To brush up on carpentry or the piano, to take French lessons or computer courses?

In spiritual terms, it is a singularly important period. We are never more ready to plumb the depths of our religious beliefs, practices and feelings. We have life experience behind us, we are freer than ever of distractions, we are more prone than ever to examine what our lives mean — to ourselves, to our families, to God. It is a time for spiritual flowering.

This, in turn, presents the Catholic Church with a powerful challenge. It is faced with an unprecedentedly large group of members who are mature, determined and able to offer time and talent to the Church's ministry. They want opportunities for service and for leadership. They constitute a powerful and exciting resource to which the Church must respond by offering opportunities for meaningful involvement.

The Catholic Church is just beginning to become aware of the challenge and has a long way to go to respond. The Church must reach out in order to utilize the time, the resources, the energy and the good will of its older members. This is particularly true in the area of ministry.

Those who glibly write off older Catholics as opponents of change are scribbling in an ivory tower. They need to talk to older Catholics and to experience their enthusiasm for the changes in the Church. More and more older Catholics are coming to the fore to take advantage of the chance to participate more actively in the life of the Church.

But it is a two-way street: the Church must respond

and *third age* Catholics must assert themselves. They must develop greater consciousness of their stage of life and develop a greater sense of solidarity. They are not the leftover segment of the Church — after children have been taken care of and family life fostered. They are integral to the life of the Church and can have a major role.

American society, no less than the churches, faces the enormous challenge of *third age* men and women who are calling upon church and society to overcome the cult of the young and the obsession with staying young. "Senior Power" and "Gray Panther" have emerged as activist groups, as have organizations devoted to the needs, interests and goals of older Americans.

It is a welcome sign that "gray" Americans are standing up against the stereotypes, the jokes and the outright signs of discrimination in jobs. For one thing, as surveys show repeatedly, so-called "old people" don't see themselves as "old."

Of course, there are older people who succumb to the prejudice of ageism and say, "Nobody cares about me or about what I feel, say and do." But there are more and more who recognize the opportunities of the *third age*. They are saying things like:

"Boy, am I glad to be out of the rat race! I can call my own shots."

"Now, I'm free to do many things that I have always wanted to do."

"My responsibilities and obligations are not pressing in on me as before. I'm able to do what I couldn't do before."

"It's wonderful! Now I can do something different with my life."

The *third age*, then, represents an opportunity to use greater independence and freedom to draw upon experience and knowledge to make choices — conscious ones. *Third age* people can say to themselves: "I have been around a good number of years now and have developed a certain wisdom and understanding. I have a better idea than ever before who I am and what matters for me. I have measured my values against life and I can figure out better than ever what I want to do with the rest of my life."

One basic fact emerges: at an age when life was over in the past, life can have a new beginning today.

What does this mean for the individual man and woman?

It means every person in the *third age* of life recognizes that each period of life has its own opportunities and challenges, just as it has distinctive liabilities and burdens. Men and women in the *third age* can draw new boundary lines and open themselves up to new opportunities. They have at their disposal more knowledge, experience and maturity than in the previous decades of their lives. They need only the will to find and follow the many ways to grow, develop and live a meaningful *third age* — and thereby fulfill the poet's promise that *the best is yet to be.*

TWO

Changing for the Better

THE DECADES after age 50 are a time for change and growth, for inner and outer trips, for exploring new avenues of satisfaction and rediscovering the satisfactions of familiar activities. It can and should be an age of fulfillment.

To a large extent, this positive and promising view of life in the *third age* revolves around how we respond to the twin pillars of personal economics and activity — work and retirement.

First, we must clear away false assumptions like the following albatrosses:

§ FALSE: Work always means a full-time job, particularly the same old job.

§ FALSE: Years after 50 are not meant to be a time of searching, exploring and experimenting.

§ FALSE: Status and a prestige position equal personal satisfaction and fulfillment.

§ FALSE: Age 65 is a fixed, immutable point in our personal firmament that dictates what we can and cannot do.

§ FALSE: After retiring, it is too late to try anything new or different.

Actually, at about age 50 — when children are grown and on their own, when Americans are established in job, career, family and community — a *third age* gets under way with new possibilities for working, living and gaining satisfaction. This time of life is set off from the *first* and *second ages* — the time of growing up and going to school and then the time of working, building a career, and raising a family.

More than ever in life, the *third age* can mean more options and more opportunities for making a contribution and for being fulfilled as an individual and as a religious person. The key is *both* reaching out and reaching in, inner growth and outer-directed concern for other people. The arrows of self need to point in both directions.

Personal growth involves wanting to learn more, understand more, reflect more, study more, read more and pray more than was possible previously. Distractions and pressures of job and family change and are likely to free the individual to develop personal resources and pursue individual interests.

But this is not enough. Whether we are in pre-retirement or in retirement, withdrawal and isolation from others can cause us to wither as vital human beings and responsive Christians. Rather than self-serving self-gratification, the *third age* calls for deeper involvement with others, with society and with our faith.

Where does the Gospel say anything about retiring as disengagement? Jesus spoke of blessedness as clothing the naked, feeding the hungry, reaching out as a peacemaker, comforting those who weep and rejoicing with those who rejoice.

The *third age* is a time when personal relationships are all-important. It calls for a conscious effort to develop, enrich and maintain friendships. It means placing a high priority on hospitality, which enriches us more than it enriches those who experience our hospitality. Family life in its richest moments teaches us that sharing, helping, exchanging and responding to others makes life meaningful and brings the spirit of the Gospels to life.

In the 10 to 15 years before retirement, an examination of personal interests is in order. Men and women need to consider what activity interests them most, what gives them the most satisfaction, and what they would like to spend time on. This means saying: "What is there about my work, my outside interests and my hobbies that gives me the most pleasure? How can I go about spending more of my time and energy in the years ahead on what I want to do most of all? What are my alternatives?"

Depending on the answers to those questions, people may decide to change jobs, to change careers, or to change assignments where they are working. Admittedly, in a tight economy, options are curtailed, but they are not eliminated. It takes initiative, effort and sometimes a bit of luck.

One decision about work may be early retirement. Half of the nation's manufacturing firms are looking into or now offer early retirement plans. Often, early retirees receive payments to carry them over until they receive Social Security along with their regular pension. Many companies have programs to prepare their employees for retirement on the sound theory that preparation not only makes retiring easier, but a success. Without preparation, free time becomes an enemy instead of an opportunity.

In preparing for retirement, we tend to overlook the place of work in our lives. It is not just earning money to pay the bills, enjoy a vacation, and put something aside. It is also a source of identification and of self-esteem as well as the major outlet for our energies and skills. It is the predominant social arena in which we have regular contacts with a group of people, develop friendships and enjoy the company of others.

While work has always dominated the lives of men, more and more women are involved in jobs and careers, many of them returning to work after their children grow up. Nothing brings home the significance of work as do the stories we all hear repeatedly of the man who worked hard all his life so he could reitre and go fishing — only to die suddenly soon after retiring.

After a lifetime in a job or career, work is bound to be a major part of our lives. But it should be kept in perspective, particularly when retirement lies ahead. We need to examine what we have given up in order to get the benefits of work. We need to examine the importance of work in our present stage of life and consciously seek new opportunities.

Observers have noticed the spread of a post-retirement work ethic: second and even third careers for men, new careers for women. Ed Townsend, who edits a newsletter on retirement planning, offers these guidelines:

• Decide what we want from work in a second career — income, more social contacts, a chance to follow new interests, to apply untapped talents and skills, an opportunity to serve others.

• Examine our work experience, skills, ambitions and hobbies for new directions. These often lead to discovery of a new job or career.

• Search for new possibilities by reading and by talking to other people. The library is a good place to start.

• Realize that a new direction at an older age means making an extra effort and applying imagination.

• Remember that it is never too late to try something new. Colonel Sanders did not start his fried chicken empire until he was 65. Success stories abound of older Americans who reached new heights after 65, whether in politics (S. I. Hayakawa launched his one-term Senate career at 70) or art (Grandma Moses began painting in her late 70s).

One former executive summed up his "retirement" to three new careers this way: "When I get up, I just decide if I want to be dusty or greasy or smelling like chicken." He was referring to his three business activities. He and his wife converted their hobby of collecting antiques into a business. His love of old cars led him to collect them and now he restores them for customers. In addition, he and his son went into the business of franchise chicken restaurants.

After building a beauty empire that covered six continents, Helena Rubinstein stated — in her 90s: "I believe in hard work. It keeps the wrinkles out of the mind and spirit. It helps keep a woman young. It certainly keeps a woman alive."

Pure and simple, retirement doesn't mean what it once did when people had to stop working because they were too frail to go on. When Social Security was established in 1935, the average life expectancy was 62. That made a retirement age of 65 reasonable. Today, when the average life expectancy is in the mid-70s and increasing numbers of people are living into their 80s, age 65 is meaningless as any indicator of the health and vitality of Americans. (It is projected that during this century, the number of Americans aged 65 to 73 will increase by 57 percent, those 75 to 84 by 57 percent, those 85 and over by 91 percent.)

Retirement is no longer viewed as a way of taking care of people who have worked long and hard and cannot go on, but rather as a reward for "veteranship." In fact, there is a distinct trend toward early retirement for a mixture of reasons. Among many employees, it is a way of getting their "reward" early. (When Sears, Roebuck & Co. offered early retirement, expecting 33 percent of those eligible to accept, it was surprised to find 60 percent accepted the opportunity.)

The trend toward finding some kind of work after retirement reflects the importance of work in our lives as well as economic pressures. Whether or not people plan to work after retiring, the essential operating principle is to stay active physically, intellectually and socially. Getting involved and applying ourselves are vital. *If you don't use what you have, you will lose it.*

A heartwarming sign of the determination to keep growing is the number of older people going back to school. Many start in the pre-retirement years to attend special classes, extension courses and training institutes in order to retool. After retiring, many others begin by going back to school — either to learn a new skill or for the sheer satisfaction of learning.

To sit in Fordham University's classrooms for "College at 60" is to experience the joy of learning and the excitement of education. Men and women in their 60s, 70s and 80s sit alongside students young enough to be their grandchildren, even their great grandchildren. The room overflows with life.

In addition, there are many opportunities for service activities by older men and women. These come in many forms: volunteer, paid, part-time, full-time. Often, people find new ways to apply their interests and their know-how. Or they discover talents and interests that they weren't previously aware of.

In Long Island, Sylvia Baron personifies the way in which variety becomes the spice of the *third age*. She retired early as a school teacher: "I wanted to see what else I could do." The *what else* included consumer affairs volunteer; consumer advocate for public television; senior intern for a U.S. Senator, and teacher in a theater workshop for retired professionals. Then she started publishing a magazine of prose and poetry written by older men and women. She is amazed at the number of people past 60 who want to be published, some of them writing from as far away as India and Wales. "Some who are 97 want to see their work in print," she reports. "One woman who submitted a poem added the postscript, 'I want you to be honest. I'm 90 and I can take it.'"

A common thread runs through the lives of men and women thriving in their *third age* of life: they are living in the active, not the passive, tense. They take charge of their lives, accept responsibility for themselves as much as they can and avoid drifting. They pay attention to their mental and physical health. They realize that living fully in the *third age* means taking into account two facts of life:

1. American society has not worked out a place for its growing population of men and women in their mature years. Individuals must find their own places.

2. Not being as young as we once were means we cannot take chances with our physical and mental well-being. Youthful myths of personal invincibility have vanished.

Often, changing for the better involves changing old habits, particularly bad habits. It always means maintaining and developing good habits. It means:

§ Getting proper medical care by finding a physician who is open and caring and by having a physical exam once a year. Early detection can bring prompt remedies and treatment that enable us to stay active.

§ Exercising regularly. Not everyone has been caught up in the physical fitness movement characterized by jogging. But it is never too late to join in. One exercise program at the University of Southern California demonstrated that 70-year-old men taking part in a year-long experiment developed the physical fitness of 40-year-olds. Of course, a physical checkup, particularly a heart examination, must precede any exercise program, which should proceed on a gradual, step-by-step basis.

§ Maintaining a proper balance of rest and activity. Excessive activity is no way of living. Neither is sleeping the day away. Knowing boundaries and dealing with them realistically are signs that *third age* men and women are shaping their lives for the better.

§ Eating properly. The older we get the higher the price we pay on the bathroom scale and in our sense of well-being when we eat too much and/or devour the wrong foods. The hardest weight to lose is weight gained after 50, since as we get older we burn off calories more slowly.

Overdoing "it" — whether it is food, drink, work, sleep or exercise — means going in the wrong direction. It means changing for the worse. So it makes sense to watch out for bad habits by taking into account our individual tendencies. Dr. Maria Guttadauria of Kings County Hospital Center in New York makes the point that "individuals have different tendencies to overdo it."

Psychologist Herbert J. Freudenberger advises men and women over 50 to *listen* to family and friends. They can be an early-warning system of overdoing it. Three steps are involved in beginning to deal with bad habits: identifying, recognizing and admitting them.

Based on what medical and mental health specialists advise, here is a sound strategy:

Talk over concerns about overdoing it with trusted family members and friends.

Visit the family physician to get a medical reading of the situation and professional guidance.

Consult with clergy, specialists at social agencies, even turn to professional counseling where necessary.

In particular, the *third age* is a time for rediscovering the importance of people in our lives — those closest to us and those in the wider circles of friendship, neighborhood and community. The more we rediscover this foundation of a meaningful and fulfilling life the more we change for the better.

This begins at home. Relationships with spouses, parents, children and blood relations in general can flourish anew with tending. They should not come to our attention only at major family events — whether weddings or funerals. They should be a conscious part of life in the *third age*.

This extends outward toward those we have daily contact with as friends and neighbors. It extends further to those we have been close to the past. Where are they now? And why aren't they in our lives today? Here is an opportunity to take a second look at the Christmas card list and move beyond mechanical greetings once a year. Or to reach out further, seeking long-lost friends.

For Catholics, the parish provides a ready-made framework for reaching out and becoming more involved with others. From serving as lectors to serving as officers of parish societies, *third age* men and women can find meaning and fulfillment in parish involvement and participation. The parish as an ongoing structure exists for its parishioners, but it can only come alive if the parishioners participate in its life and share their own lives.

The parish is also an appropriate setting where people can get together to discuss the impact of retirement on both husband and wife, whether or not both were working. Parishes can make a great contribution by establishing pre-retirement programs so that people in the same boat can discuss what they face. Ideally, retired people would participate, thereby sharing their experiences and know-how.

Such parish-based programs would be an ideal place to reach beyond pre-retirement programs that limit their focus to money and leisure. It is a matter of less money and more time and what to do about each. Certainly, these are major concerns and should be dealt with. There is also a fundamental question of values in life and personal commitment — the basis for adjusting and making life decisions in the *third age.*

In such a setting, men and women can confront their attitudes on work, status, prestige and money. They can move toward defining what power means and how responsibility is defined. They can share with others the process of sorting out their past, present and future. They can find out what counts for others and they can identify what counts for them. They can learn to "read" their own autobiographies and they can develop greater perspective on their own lives. In such ways can we speak of acquiring wisdom.

In general, priorities can change for the better. Titles, honors and high rank become less dominant. Activities become more highly valued for their own sake, less dependent on tangible rewards. Increasingly, intrinsic value and merit overshadow the externals of prizes, paychecks and diplomas.

The capacity to appreciate internal satisfaction is a sign of maturity. Then we focus on what really matters in this life: who we really are, what we stand for, what we create and what we do for others. We come to appreciate doing things that no one will ever see us do. But we see and know what we do, and so does God.

With maturity, title and status matter less and less. The substance of our activities and the consequences of our actions matter more. Increasingly, the psychological side of work becomes its intrinsic value in the doing and in the positive value to others. The creative side of work becomes preeminent, wherein we use our skills, energies, experiences and knowledge to make something, help someone or solve a problem.

In this way, the theological dimension of work is added to its practical and psychological dimensions. We become part of the work of creation and perceive not only our work but our lives as part of God's work in the world. Then the meaning of work, pre-retirement, and retirement is absorbed into the larger meaning of our lives as Christians responding to the world.

THREE

Opening Up Family Life

A STORY of two sisters personifies old and new accents in family life and the difference between open and closed attitudes toward familial relationships as the over-50 population explosion takes place.

One sister reaches beyond the confines of her immediate family. She is active in her parish, neighborhood and community — volunteering, helping, visiting, joining in. Her latest involvement centers on helping the families of recent immigrants adjust to American life.

Her activities cast a wide net to other older people, to the needy in her parish, to those who are involved in organizations, to those who are forced to stay at home. Her age? It is not significant. She is involved and never more so than when she retired. (Actually, she is in her 80s but looks in her 60s or even her 50s.)

The other sister has narrowed her world to immediate family, shutting off the outside world and extended relationships. She is over-involved with nieces and nephews, interfering with and complicating everyone's life, including her own. She has drawn a tight family circle around her life and huddled inside.

With the ever-increasing number of men and women living longer and more active lives, a more Christian view of "family" is emerging. It is extending outward toward all relationships that involve caring for and loving others. A paradox emerges. At the same time as the traditional family is embracing more living generations than ever before, there are more older Americans — particularly women — without families.

What is happening is rooted in a set of remarkable facts unprecedented in American history:

• Half of all married women in the United States will be either separated, widowed or divorced by the time they are 50.

• For those over 65, 45 percent of the women live alone, compared with 15 percent of the men. The major reason for the difference is the statistical fact that on an average, women live seven years longer than men. For every widower, there are six widows.

• Those who reach age 65 today can expect, according to government statistics, to live to age 81.

• Married couples who have expended themselves in raising families face a dramatic change in their lives. They face some 25 years with an "empty nest" — their children are grown and on their own.

• The four-generation family — alive and well — is no longer unusual and will become more prevalent. This means that families will have many more branches on the living tree.

• At the same time, 20 percent of women over 65 have no children; another 20 percent have only one child.

What all this means is that family life is no longer as simple as a *Saturday Evening Post* cover by Norman Rockwell. It does not mean that the family as the essential building block of society is finished. It means the opposite. Family is more important than ever, but we must recognize new circumstances and new opportunities for experiencing the values of family life.

The starting point is the realization that the *third*

age of life is a time for others as well as for ourselves. It is an exciting, enriching time for reaching out to others. This reaching out takes us toward fulfillment as individuals, as human beings and as Christians. It is a time to be responsive to others inside and outside the traditional family.

For married people, the process begins in the relationship between husband and wife. As the demands of job, of career and of raising children diminish, there is more time for the marital relationship. Also, there can be more strain on it.

In the *third age*, husbands and wives cannot escape easily into the roles of fathers and mothers, breadwinners and homemakers, and thereby evade the challenge of building a loving, sharing relationship that combines intimacy and independence. Husbands and wives face these challenges:

How do we leave each other room to grow?

How do we foster autonomy and still remain close?

How can we be both together and separate?

How do we respect each other's independence, while using the greater opportunities to foster closeness?

Clearly, this means that husband and wife must get to know each other all over again. This means opening up lines of communication. Couples need to identify their priorities as individuals and as a couple. It is a time of reassessment and rediscovery.

In practice, this means openness to change in their lives — by moving, by traveling, by going back to school, by starting a new career on the side and even taking up a new full-time career, by getting involved in social action, by becoming active in parish and church in newer, more demanding roles. For the individual married couple, this literally means opening their door to the world so that their concept of family is not only the narrow nuclear family, but a family of many different others that would also count in their lives.

Within the family itself, as parents and grandparents live longer, the spread of relationships reaches further and wider. Grandparents have grown-up grandchildren who marry and bring forth great-grandchildren. At the same time, children have not only grandparents, but great-grandparents. Whether looking from the top or the bottom of the family tree, there are many more branches that involve relationships. The family balancing act of responsibilities and relationships is becoming more complicated.

Because Americans are on the move so much, long-distance grandparenting is becoming a widespread phenomenon. Not only do married sons and daughters move far away to pursue careers, but so do parents, to a retirement area. According to the U.S. Census, almost one-half (46.4 percent) of Americans aged five and older have moved in the past five years and in the past decade the number of retired Americans who moved from one state to another increased by 54 percent.

For many grandparents, seeing their grandchildren is no longer a walk, an easy bus ride or a short car trip away. It takes planning. Trips must be arranged in advance, vacations coordinated. When grandchildren visit their grandparents, planning includes making them feel at home and arranging to do things with them. It is important to know grandchildren, to know what they like to do, and to give them a voice in planning what they will do during a visit. Conversely, when grandparents are the visitors, they must remember that it is not *their* house. The territory belongs to a grown child and his or her spouse.

In between visits, phone calls and letters keep lines of communication open. Some grandparents send audiocassettes and even videocassettes in which they talk to their grandchildren. One grandmother who likes to read to her grandchildren records her readings of children's books and sends the cassettes to grandchildren hundreds of miles away.

For children, grandparents represent a source of security as well as love. They are a living link with the past, representing continuity and standing as a sign that children are links in a family. Grandparents also satisfy curiosity about the past, about what it was like "way back then." Grandparents also provide a special kind of approval for their grandchildren. They are free of the ups and downs of daily parenting. They can see and appreciate their grandchildren from a more relaxed perspective than can parents. Meanwhile, young children experience their parents as models of how grown children treat their parents.

This is dramatized in care of the elderly. Comparisons with traditional society on this matter miss a major point. In the past, not many parents survived long enough to have many years as grandparents. Few lasted long enough to become grandparents of grownups. Moreover, in traditional societies, the older members held the property and controlled the wealth. Today, age is hardly a guarantor of greater wealth and power in the family. In fact, men and women entering the *third age* characteristically have parents still living and feel the responsibility of being helpful — with the amount of economic need and practical assistance varying from family to family.

Researchers have confirmed what most of us observe: rarely do grown children turn their backs on parents in need. As Dr. Stanley Cath, an expert at Tufts University Medical School, notes, "The myth of the abandoned elder is just that — a myth." He adds: "Many middle-aged parents find themselves caught between the generations — the needs of their parents and children. And some people are getting so old that it is their grandchildren who must assume the caretaking role.''

When one parent dies, their grown children face a painful decision. Sons and daughters who themselves are in the *third age* of life must decide whether to bring a surviving parent under their roof. As children grow up and move out, their parents face the prospect of moving in the older generation.

Clearly, there is no simple guideline to cover such a situation. In general, letting a parent remain in familiar surroundings works best — all other factors being equal. Uprooting creates strains for the surviving parents and strains the family life of the grown child and his or her spouse.

To view bringing parents under the same roof as the only alternative is to overlook all the other relationships that sustain us — friends, immediate neighbors, fellow volunteers and parishioners, long-time associates and colleagues. There are also newer relationships, epitomized by the wonderful program of foster grandparents. Uprooting can create more problems than it solves.

For the many women in the *third age* who live alone or with other women their age, helping others enlarges their emotional and psychological support system. They look in on each other, keep track of each other, do things together. They know they are there for each other — certainly a familylike relationship.

Within parish life, pastors are noticing that daily Mass has become the focal point for ongoing relationships between parishioners. Regular Mass-goers learn each other's names, become friendly, exchange recipes and remedies, begin to do things together. If someone doesn't show up at Mass one morning, parishioners immediately get on the phone to make sure nothing is wrong, to see whether any help is needed. The caring congregation at such daily Masses is the embodiment of Christian community that makes the Church the center for human relationships.

"Senior citizen housing" — as it is called — is another example of an informal family grouping. Such housing is not for everyone, but for those who choose it, a new framework of relationships develops. Residents share each other's interests, activities, problems and pleasures. They stimulate one another intellectually, care for one another, assist one another, develop ongoing relationships. It is also another form of family life.

In various parts of the country, older homeowners living alone are sharing their homes. Arrangements vary from renting part of the house to exchange of services for a room. More than economics is involved as owner and tenant develop a sense of responsibility for each other. An older homeowner may share with another older person or with a younger adult. This is done in various cities with the assistance of special organizations such as Philadelphia Match or Action for Better Living for Elders (ABLE) in San Francisco.

An example of the bonding that occurs is explained by a 24-year-old sociology student who lives in a two-room suite of a home owned by a 75-year-old retired teacher in Philadelphia. He contributes $200 each year toward the gas bill and does routine household chores. "I feel like it's my home too," he reports. "I have an emotional investment."

In more than 125 U.S. locations, adults are living in large, self-run cooperative homes that encompass men and women from their 20s to their 80s. They share costs, household chores, eat together at least once a week and make group decisions on running the house. In Boston, for example, at the Shared Living House, 14 adults ranging from 21 to 84 constitute a "housing family." They have a feeling of family togetherness as they turn the house they share into a home.

Throughout the *third age*, men and women are reaching out to link up with *significant others* without confining themselves to the boundaries of the traditional family. It is not only a necessity. It is a human and Christian outreach that proclaims the fullness of their involvement in the life all around them. Sometimes, this produces misunderstanding and a negative reaction among members of their own family. It is a form of the prejudice of ageism when other family members expect *third age* men and women to retreat and withdraw instead of reaching out. Relatives all but come out and say *"Act your age,"* which translates into a tyrannical demand that older adults let age dictate what they do and how they feel. It is a way of trying to slam the door on the outside world and on people outside the immediate family.

The most pointed instance of such an attitude arises when widowed parents decide to remarry. Grown sons and daughters can act as though they never heard of the facts of life; they act as if parents should stay on the shelf and get pushed further back out of the mainstream of life. Lesser versions of this prejudice may crop up when parents of grown children want to make changes in their lives — from getting involved in new interests to moving.

A reciprocal right should be operating. Just as grown children have the right to their own autonomy, so do their parents. Just as parents cannot realistically expect to get all their fulfillment within the confines of their immediate families, neither can their families expect parents to confine themselves to their immediate families.

When men and women in the *third age* reach out and share themselves with others, they are energizing their family relations, themselves and all those they come into contact with. The family epitomizes close relationships in which people care for each other in all the meanings of the word — economically, emotionally and spiritually. Insofar as new accents in the meaning of family relationships develop, the meaning of family will be enriched, as will men and women in the *third age*.

FOUR
Renewing Marriage

MARRIED couples in their 50s and 60s are writing a new chapter in the book of marriage. Never before have so many Americans faced the opportunities and challenges of living together for 10 to 30 years after fulfilling the main responsibilities of family life. Not only that, but they have better health, more leisure and greater freedom than in past generations. The *third age* couple today can evolve a new togetherness as husband and wife. They have more time for each other and for individual development than they had in the first two decades of their married life. It is a time for marriage renewal.

The potential for fulfilling togetherness depends on greater attention to each other's interests and needs: more sharing, and increased sensitivity to what a spouse wants out of life. Instead of being preoccupied with family responsibilities, husband and wife can become occupied with their individual selves within the context of the marriage partnership.

Husbands and wives in the *third age* make comments like: "You know, we forgot how much the two of us enjoyed going downtown together" . . . . "It was nothing special, but sneaking off to a movie, the two of us alone, was just great" . . . . "This year we are going to pick our own vacation spot and make our own plans — just for us" .... "We are once again discovering the pleasure of each other's company."

But husbands and wives must heed the porcupine analogy that marriage and family counselors cite in underlining the importance of balancing closeness and independence. According to the analogy, two porcupines tried to keep each other warm on a very cold winter's day. But when they came too close, they hurt each other with their quills. When they moved too far apart, they were cold. They had to adjust in such a way that they were close enough to warm each other, but not so close as to stab each other with their quills.

Possessiveness means getting too close.

Inertia can keep a couple too far apart.

When couples look only to each other for company, for activities and for sharing interests, they cut themselves off from the many opportunities all around them. They limit personal growth and restrict what they have to offer each other. They shortchange themselves and each other.

At a time when women have entered the work force in such numbers and when more and more women are going back to work after their children grow up, husbands must adjust to a new reality. (Over half the female population is working.) Wives no longer can be automatically expected to be keeping house at the beck and call of husbands.

The husband who fails to take into account his wife's activities expects her to be around all the time. "What's going on?" he asks. "Isn't being a wife good enough for you?" To which the wife has an answer: "Wife, yes. Twenty-four-hour housewife, no."

Here, there is a risk of confusion. The traditional roles of wife, mother and homemaker are not being put down. Not at all. That is not the point, as women have been telling men. The point is having the choice and not being forced into an automatic pigeonhole. When children are grown and the demands of home-making decline significantly, women often feel the need and have the opportunity to go to work. At that stage, many other wives have already made the choice, frequently out of economic necessity.

Husbands who downplay the working lives of their spouses put a damper on the marital relationship. Without fully realizing it, they may try to restrict the activities of their wives. For their part, wives may do the same thing when their husbands develop new interests in hobbies, special courses, volunteer work. From whatever direction, possessiveness can have a devastating effect on *third age* couples.

The other problem — inertia — has different forms. Taking each other for granted is the most obvious. When a couple have been there for each other for many years and have gone through life's ups and downs together, they assume that they know what each other wants, thinks, feels. They may never ask or try to find out.

The tendency is to say: "If two people get married, they share ideals, values, interests, and over the years they share and share alike, getting more and more in tune with each other. And so it goes." As a result, we have celebrated stability rather than change within human relationships.

Borrowing a page from Marriage Encounters is a sound idea. At Encounter weekends, husband and wife go apart from each other and reflect systematically on what is important for each personally. They write it all down and then they compare each other's inventory. The procedure is not only suited to young couples. Older couples need to confront the changes in their interests, needs, and priorities and compare notes.

Often, a husband or wife will look up in surprise, and

say, "I didn't know that you liked . . . . Why didn't you ever say so before?" In the background, there is the shattering response, "You never asked or bothered to find out."

Finding out about each other in an open, seeking, mutually supportive way is the basis of new togetherness for *third age* couples. It is a psychological renewal of the marital relationship, a clear sign of commitment and of concern for each other.

In a real sense, it harkens back to the courtship stage when a young couple discover each other. In the *third age*, they seek each other out as mature and experienced individuals. What they see will be clearer and richer when seen with the eyes of mutual love and commitment. There will be less fantasy, more reality; fewer romanticized expectations, but better odds on behaving wisely and well.

This calls for a readiness to talk things out with loving honesty. This involves acceptance of the other and respect for what he or she wants and needs. This requires open lines of communication so that each partner feels down deep that the other is listening, really listening.

Dr. Sven Wahlroos, a prominent clinical psychologist, has reported after decades of treating families in trouble that the "main reason for the discord is simply that the consciously felt love and the good intentions harbored by the family members are not communicated in such a way that they are recognized."

When communication breaks down, both speaker and listener, sender and receiver are at fault. It takes two to communicate and in the process listening is the crucial ingredient. It is also the highest compliment that one person can pay another. Listening speaks much louder than words in saying to another: "You are really important to me, so important that I will listen to what you have to say." At the other extreme, the severest putdown is the attitude, "I've heard all this before."

A common mistake between husband and wife is to view communications as strictly informational. As often as not, a spouse is sending a message about his or her feelings wrapped in facts or in a story about a routine incident. The challenge is to register those feelings by noting tone of voice, facial expressions, body language and general mood. It is important to look for the context of what is said and to recall similar episodes. Is the mood different? In what ways? What is going on in our lives at this time? In our marriage?

Carl Rogers, the celebrated psychologist, has described what it means to listen fully to someone else:

> "When I say that I enjoy hearing someone, I mean, of course, hearing deeply. I mean that I hear the words, the thoughts, the feeling tones, the personal meaning, even the meaning that is below the conscious intent of the speaker. Sometimes too, in a message which superficially is not very important, I hear a deep human cry that lies buried and unknown far below the surface of the person.
>
> "So I have learned to ask myself, can I hear the sounds and sense the shape of this other person's inner world? Can I resonate to what he is saying so deeply that I sense the meanings he is afraid of yet would like to communicate, as well as those he knows?" (Carl R. Rogers, *A Way of Being*, Houghton Mifflin Company [Boston, 1980] p.8).

Husbands and wives in the *third age* need to ask themselves, *How many times am I listening in this way to the special person in my life, to my lifelong mate?*

Dr. Rogers has devised a simple test of whether or not we are *really* listening to someone else. It is particularly useful during an argument or disagreement by providing immediate feedback on whether the two parties are getting their message across. The test has only one rule: you can only answer other persons *after* you have restated in your own words what they have said to *their* satisfaction. Dr. Rogers comments: "Sounds simple doesn't it? But if you try it you discover it is one of the most difficult things you have ever tried to do."

Without listening, communication fails.

Without communication, sharing doesn't materialize.

Without sharing, togetherness is a facade.

Husbands and wives in the *third age* need to pay particular attention to the time they spend together. Do they give themselves opportunities to communicate with each other in meaningful ways? Or:

Is the television set on all the time, even during dinner?

Do they always go out with other couples? Never alone, the two of them?

Do they feel uncomfortable when they are alone together?

Do they focus their attention on grown children and grandchildren to the exclusion of each other?

Do they keep doing the same things in the same old way, whether it is a night out, vacations or entertaining?

When critical moments arise, couples are forced to pay attention to each other, but unless lines of communication are kept open they will have trouble being direct with each other. Instead of discussing an issue they face, they may veer into an argument about the past or get sidetracked in mutual accusations. Instead of a constructive exchange, they will take fixed positions. Instead of understanding, they will have misunderstandings. Instead of working together toward a decision, they will argue with each other.

On the other hand, husbands and wives with open lines of communication in a loving relationship help each other to clarify thinking and to deal with feelings. They provide mutual support and reinforcement. They share what they know and offer insights into each other's feelings. They are able to reach a joint decision that satisfactorily meets the needs of both husband and wife without forcing one or the other to surrender. Each time this happens a *third age* couple renews and energizes the marital relationship.

Decision-making is a major test. These include choices on where to work, live, vacation; on when to retire, on relations with grown children, on what to do with family finances. What affects both partners must be discussed by both in order to strengthen their togetherness. Such sharing builds harmony instead of creating resentment.

In the *third age*, particularly as more women are working, couples find themselves changing the way they share power and household duties. Husbands are sharing their control of the family finances and making joint decisions on both spending and investing family funds. The wife's control of relations with grown children and grandchildren is taking into account the husband's wants and feelings. Husbands are learning about running the household, wives about managing finances. (The latter is particularly important, given the longer life expectancy of women).

Greater togetherness in the *third age* is characterized by a stronger sense of partnership and greater mutual respect. Strict segregation of powers and duties yields to mutual participation. Husband and wife develop a new appreciation of each other and discover new dimensions and possibilities in each other. They see each other with fresh eyes and invariably they like what they see.

Third age couples need to ask themselves:

Do we both enjoy this house or apartment as much as we once did?

Do we still enjoy living in this neighborhood? Does it still have the same advantages for us? Are we ignoring the drawbacks? Or are we failing to appreciate the many attractions?

Are we seeing the friends we really enjoy?

Are we spending our leisure time in ways that give us the most satisfaction?

Are we able to disagree and come to a conclusion without ill feelings?

Must one of us always have his or her way? Are we both able to make reasonable compromises?

Are we able to discuss our fears and our hopes?

Do we enjoy a good laugh together from time to time? If not, why not?

Do I help my mate to grow?

As retirement approaches in the *third age*, both husband and wife need to discuss future plans and the adjustments involved. This becomes particularly complicated when the husband retires and the wife, who often started working within the past 10 years, continues to hold down a job. Usually younger than her husband, the wife is on a different job timetable. So a new phenomenon is emerging in *third age* marriages: retired husbands with working wives.

A role reversal of this kind can take couples by surprise if they don't discuss it openly in advance. A professor of psychiatry at Mount Sinai School of Medicine in New York, Dr. Joel Wallack, warns that the role reversal can be jarring. "Some women may feel they've abandoned their husbands," he warns. "And with that guilt, they may feel anger at the husband for creating this emotional burden."

Dr. Wallack's suggestion fits the theme of open communication and sharing in marriage: "Retirement is never easy. It is important that both parties assess the effect the change is going to have on their lives. They should find time to do things together to reshape the relationship in terms of new interests that they can share and both feel successful at."

In the process of renewing marriage in the *third age*, the habit of keeping everything to oneself stands in the way of meaningful sharing. This is much easier to acknowledge than to act on. Sometimes, it helps to draw on the experiences and advice of a third party, as we do in our spiritual lives with a spiritual director or confessor. The third party can be a trusted and respected friend. In many companies, counselors are available, particularly for pre-retirement planning. Specialists such as marriage counselors are certainly of great value when husband and wife feel as though they have reached a dead end. In whatever direction we turn, the very process of talking things over helps us to see both our situations and ourselves in perspective.

For the Christian couple in the *third age,* prayer plays an important role. Prayer is not only an intensely personal matter or a formal liturgical activity. For the mature couple, an extemporaneous sharing of prayer brings a powerful force into their lives. Not a large number of words are needed, nor formulas, but a deep and personal sharing — while doing the dishes, walking down the street hand-in-hand, sitting by the fire or having a cup of coffee in the kitchen.

It is appropriate for a couple to acknowledge the things for which they're grateful — the gift of faith, the joys of their children, the daily pleasures of living, the satisfaction of their life together. To take such things into account together and then to seek God's guidance is to sanctify everyday activities.

The praying could be a conversation in which they invite the Lord to be present. They are saying to each other, "Let's not permit the reality of our lives to slip by unnoticed. Let's stand back for a few moments to share our reflections with the Lord and invite Him to be present." While this can emerge spontaneously, it is also a sound idea to set aside a specific time to pray out of the fullness of the relationship.

When people ask for a quick way of identifying a *third age* couple who are thriving in their togetherness, a clearcut sign is hospitality. Not only members of the family, but neighbors enjoy stopping by, from the pre-schooler to the elderly.

Hospitality involves a certain amount of risk, since we are not always going to find the experience satisfying or our guests responsive. Meanwhile, however, we are making an important statement: that we have confidence in ourselves and other human beings, that we value people and human company, that we are open to others, to change, to the I-Thou relationship.

Friendship, hospitality, mutual attentiveness, joint prayer — all these elements in the *third age* celebrate the fundamental need to reach out to others, to each other and to God. In giving of ourselves, we gain the enrichment of getting close to others.

The larger the circle of people and interests that the *third age* couple draw around themselves, the richer and more solid is the nucleus composed of the two of them. Then their togetherness is richer and deeper and they grow individually as they grow closer together.

FIVE

Staying Active

A STOCKROOM worker, a cardiologist, a financial specialist and a modelmaker tell the same tale of what to do with the increasing amounts of free time that becomes available in the *third age*, particularly with retirement: *Stay Active.*

"I don't know where the time has gone," reports Charles Phillips several years after retiring from the stockroom of an Illinois engineering firm. "When I first thought of retirement, I made up my mind to go into volunteer work. . . . I've worked as a teacher's helper, tutoring in math, reading and spelling. I work two days a week, five hours a day. The kids call me Charlie. They call my wife Mrs. Charlie. . . . People can make of retirement what they want. If they want to sit in a rocking chair they can do it. If they want to be active, there are so many things to do."

Retiring after 51 years as a cardiologist, Dr. Don Carlos Peete from Kansas advises: "You must be interested in life. You just can't sit on the sidelines and watch the world go by. . . . I advise people to have a prayer in the morning to handle situations that come up during the day, and to be patient about it. But they have to do that in the morning. They can't wait until the situation presents itself."

In Florida, where she works at a marine laboratory,

Lucille Wasserman notes that her 30-year career on Wall Street did "nothing to prepare me for the challenges of retirement years." Although she herself has moved to a retirement area, she advises, "If at all possible, don't cut your bridges to what you've done and where you've been." To guide herself, she cites a Hindu prayer: "God give me work for the rest of my life, and life for the rest of my work."

In Massachusetts, former modelmaker Allen B. Metcalfe retired from his job at Polaroid Corporation and became a jeweler: "I'm a very happy person. If I had known it would be like this, I would have retired 20 years ago. . . . I learned about stones and mountings — malachite, jasper, crazy-lace agate, opal, tiger eye, African sodalite. I learned about ivory and scrimshaw. I made pendants, belt buckles, earrings, bracelets, rings. All my orders are word of mouth. When I retired, my friends gave me two fishing reels — salt water and fresh water. I've been too busy to use either one." (Quoted in "Retirement: The New Beginning" by Marilyn Gardner, *The Christian Science Monitor*, 1981 Reprint, pages 6-7.)

Stockroom worker, cardiologist, financial specialist, modelmaker, all were describing variations on the best single prescription for longer, healthier and happier lives in the *third age*: activity. It is the ounce of prevention that dramatically reduces the chances of becoming physically frail, mentally sluggish, psychologically depressed and socially isolated. For committed Christians, religious activity in parish life and personal spiritual exercises sustain and nourish their inner life of faith and hope. In this way, the active life not only fulfills them in human terms, it is their Christian witness. Activity then lights up the world of others as well as their own lives.

The *third age* is decidedly not a time for

retrenching and for pulling back from life. It actually presents more opportunities for reaching out to others and for becoming involved. With more options and fewer demands from the outside, it is a period of choice. Activity no longer is dictated by job and family in the same way it once was. The *third age* calls for more attention to the decisions on what to do with time and energy. More than ever in life, activity is purposeful and it can be more satisfying than ever before. It is also "a biological necessity," as emphasized by the world-renowned biologist, Dr. Hans Selye.

He speaks for experts and specialists in a wide range of disciplines in stressing the importance of activity:

> To keep fit, we must exercise both our bodies and our minds. Besides inactivity deprives us of every outlet for our innate urge to create, to build; this causes tensions and the insecurity that stems from aimlessness. Whether we call our activity exhausting work or relaxing play depends largely upon our own attitude toward it. We should at least get on friendly terms with our job; ideally, we should try to find "play professions" that are as pleasant, useful, and constructive as possible. These should give us the best outlets — safety valves — for self-realization, and for preventing irrational, violent outbreaks or flight into the dream life of drugs such as occur in people whose high motivation is frustrated by the lack of an acceptable aim. In seeking a worthwhile goal, remember my little jingle: "*Fight for your highest attainable aim, but never put up resistance in vain.*"
>
> Remember also that, in most instances, diversion from one activity to another is more relaxing than complete rest. Few things are as frustrating as complete inactivity, the absence of any stimuli or any challenge, to which you could react. (Hans Selye, *Stress*

Without Distress, New American Library Signet Book/New York, 1975/pp. 136-7.)

This is the proper focus for viewing the process of getting older instead of an undermining emphasis on disabilities that may or may not come with age. Actually, for every person over 65 who is disabled, there is a disabled person under 65. While it is obviously true that the chances of becoming disabled increase with age, we must beware of generalizing. There are 70-year-old marathon runners and 40-year-olds without enough breath to run for a bus at the corner. Men and women can become "old" at 50 or 80. Though the body's physiological systems begin to decline after our late 20s, the rate and pace vary from one individual to another, and the body, as well as the mind, has incredible resiliency.

Dr. Robert N. Butler indicts "the myth of *aging itself*, the idea of chronologic aging, measuring one's age by the number of years one has lived." He adds: "It is clear that there are great differences in the rates of physiologic, chronologic, psychologic and social aging from person to person and also within each individual."

All of us are getting older all the time, but at different rates. Circumstances differ from one person to another and for each individual from year to year. Each of us is writing an individual autobiography where change and adjustment represent a law of life. Each of us has the task of identifying our strengths and potential and of drawing on them to continue growing throughout our lives.

The truism already cited is worth repeating: *If we don't use it, we'll lose it.* Unless we apply our physical, mental and social capabilities they will deteriorate from disuse — as they can from misuse. So also with our religious needs. We can never stop discovering and rediscovering God in our lives, we always need to seek new manifestations of the Divine Presence.

First of all, on the physical side, the *third age* of life benefits from sound living habits and from medical progress. In giving up smoking, watching weight and exercising regularly, Americans are developing a remarkable track record in taking care of their health. The concern about everything from stress to food additives underscores the widespread acceptance of the fact that the way we live shapes our physical well-being. We also harvest the benefits throughout our lives.

Meanwhile, modern medicine rescues us from sicknesses that were once debilitating and even fatal, while making it easier to live with a variety of ailments. From heart disease to chronic arthritis, Americans of every age are able to lead normal lives that would otherwise have been seriously disrupted only 20 or 30 years ago.

To counter the onslaught of heart disease, doctors have a dramatic set of responses: new diagnostic techniques, heart bypass surgery, artificial pacemakers and heart valve implants, and drugs for hypertension, congestive heart failure, angina, and arrhythmia. People who only a few years ago were crippled by arthritis now move about without pain and even go skiing and play tennis.

Without any doubt, the news on the medical front is encouraging and exciting, but we only reap the benefits by taking care of ourselves and by maintaining a regular and reasonable amount of physical activity. The amount depends on the individual, but the universal rule calls for regular exercise. This helps to maintain muscle tone, particularly the heart muscle, to improve circulation and breathing, to control weight and to ease tension. Particular emphasis should be placed on activities that increase the efficiency of heart and lungs, such as swimming, bike riding and brisk walking.

A study conducted at the University of California in Los Angeles pinpointed seven basic habits to stay healthy:

- Never smoke cigarettes.
- Get regular physical activity.
- Use alcohol moderately or never.
- Sleep seven to eight hours per night.
- Maintain proper weight.
- Eat breakfast.
- Avoid eating between meals.

The researchers found in studying 7,000 people over a 10-year period that the life expectancy of a 45-year-old man who followed all seven rules was 11 years longer than those who followed three or fewer.

Staying mentally active calls for involvement with outside stimuli. It is impossible to thrive in isolation. We need contact with others in order to exchange ideas, reactions, opinions and conclusions. Other people respond to our views and, in turn, stimulate us. This is not the same as holding forth as an opinionated monologuist who only talks to hear the sound of his or her own voice. For others to listen to us we must be willing and able to listen to others.

There are many ways to stay mentally active, but all ways are built on interest in the world around us. Each person points that interest in individual and particular directions. What is needed is an intake of information from the media, from reading, from other people, from lectures, special courses and study groups. Or going back to school can open up new and challenging frontiers.

Whether it is the news of the day or the news of the neighborhood, curiosity involves an interest in life — our own and others'. Eleanor Roosevelt, herself a prime example of lifelong curiosity, put it so well: "Life was meant to be lived, and curiosity must be kept alive. One must never, for whatever reason, turn his back on life."

For more and more people, the *third age* is a time to pursue new interests now that time and opportunity present themselves. This also means going out and finding such opportunities in the neighborhood, parish and larger community. Asking friends and neighbors and visiting libraries, community centers and local schools brings in a long list of possibilities.

Both the famous and the not-so-famous demonstrate the fruits of continued productivity over the years. General Douglas MacArthur and Winston Churchill, for example, were in their 60s and in virtual eclipse at the outbreak of World War II and then proceeded to lead and inspire the free world. In the arts, Georgia O'Keefe reached new artistic heights in her 90s; in the theater and movie world, performers like Laurence Olivier (born 1907) and George Burns (born 1896) have scorned the notion of retiring. But we don't need to look only to the famous. All around us, men and women demonstrate that they are mentally and socially productive. They have much to offer and they share it.

Increasingly, retired men and women are finding ways to demonstrate their productivity, particularly with part-time jobs as a way to keep work in their lives. It is not only for the money, which can be a factor in the face of inflation. Work also gives people a feeling of greater control over their lives, provides a sense of purpose and worth, and satisfies social needs. It enables men and women to be connected, to feel "at home" in society.

Both pre-retired and retired employees are aware of the meaning of work. Almost half (48 percent) of those 50 to 64 years old told Harris pollsters that they intend to extend their working lives. Almost as high a proportion of retirees (46 percent) said they would like to be working. This is reflected in the 16 percent increase in part-time employment among the elderly during the 1971-1981 decade.

Consultant Frank Bowe makes the point that the missing ingredient is a flexible arrangement for continuing to work after retirement. "Perhaps 75 to 80 percent of those considering retirement would keep working if they could only get their job descriptions modified to allow for more safety, diminished physical demands, and, in many cases, fewer hours," he reports. Why not give older Americans something productive to do, he argues, instead of paying them not to work?

Economist Peter F. Drucker, one of the most astute observers of American society, predicts that flexible retirement is going to be the central social issue of the next 10 years. "It is going to play the role that minority employment played in the 1960s and women's rights in the 1970s," he states.

American society faces this challenge because of the role played by work. As pointed out by E. Bentley Lipscomb of the U.S. Senate Special Committee on Aging: "We've inculcated in people from childhood on that work gives value. Then the system is set up so we take that away from them. After six months (of retirement) they've caught every fish known to man. They've played every golf course within 200 miles. After that? . . ."

Moreover, a number of studies confirm that older employees are not only productive, but have lower absenteeism, greater job stability and a more positive attitude than younger employees. Malcolm Morrison, a U.S. Department of Labor expert, points out that retaining older employees is more often a bargain than a burden.

At a company with a model attitude, Warren Publishing Corporation near Boston, eight of its 35 employees are eligible for Social Security but still work because they want to. The company lets them determine how many hours they work and, within reason, select the work they do. The company's president, Tim Warren Sr., reports, "We get tremendous value out of our older workers."

His description of their contribution has a universal ring: "When you bring young people in and put them in an environment in which they observe older people working right up to the last minute, paying attention to what they are doing — it is like parenting. This sense of responsibility, these diligent work habits, all of this is very definitely transmitted by older people to younger people. And we like it, because it makes a company a microcosm of the world — young and old, working together."

Forward-looking companies are beginning to receive this message. Control Data Corporation, Manhattan Bank, and Travelers Insurance Companies are leading the way in seeking out older employees. Some corporations even have set up special employment offices for this purpose. Mature Temps is operating nationally as an employment service for older workers. Organizations are cropping up to help older men and women find employment, such as Retirement Jobs, Inc., of San Francisco, Second Careers Program of Los Angeles, and Senior Personnel Employment Council of Westchester (New York).

Signs of changed attitudes toward older workers indicate progress in the battle against ageism. Older workers themselves demonstrate the foolishness of distorted views about the significance of year of birth. At Warren Publishing Company, 82-year-old Winifred Church is still running the mail room full-time, 40 years after starting to work. She promptly points out that age does not determine an individual's ability to be gainfully employed. Sure, she says, there are some older people who are unable to work, then adds: "I've also known some people who were pretty decrepit at the age of 30." Or as the highly-quotable baseball pitcher Satchel Paige once said: "How old would you be if you didn't know how old you was?"

The definitive report on both the physical and mental fronts as we grow older comes from Dr. Robert Butler: it "can be an emotionally healthy and satisfying time of life with a minimum of physical and mental impairment." He points out what everyone working in the field finds: "many older people have adapted well to their old age with little stress and a high level of morale."

At every part of the *third age*, morale is connected with being socially active. Never is it clearer that human beings are social animals, that people need people, that the way people feel about themselves depends on how other people feel about them. People who are alone with their television sets talk to the images on the screen. It is their last resort.

People in the *third age* usually rediscover the value of personal relationships, but often they need to add effort to awareness. They need to go out of their way to become involved with other people, by joining groups, by extending helping hands, by sharing with others, by being as active as they can.

One example, among many, comes to mind: a woman in her 80s, living in an Upper West Side New York apartment where she always rented to another elderly woman, and where she did typing for the college students in the area. Each week she worked a day at her local church doing secretarial work. She remained alive, responsive, vibrant and involved. She never lost touch with people and her morale was always high.

For the committed Christian, one's parish and church are a vital center of communication and of contact on the religious as well as spiritual level. Daily Mass becomes a vehicle for being in contact with other regular churchgoers. Church organizations offer opportunities for service and involvement. The parish is a source of identity and a reminder that they belong. Worshiping with others enables everyone — at whatever age — to affirm the deepest self that sees the image of God in others. This then becomes the most meaningful of activities that characterize an individual's active flowering in the *third age* of life.

SIX

Deciding Where to Live

THE OLDER we get the more crucial our housing arrangements become and also the more difficult it is to think of moving. It can be called the "attic syndrome": What are we going to do with all the things we have accumulated over the years? What am I going to do with the things in the attic alone? The concerns are more fundamental, of course, such as leaving behind the familiarity and security of friends, neighbors, organizations and parish. Moving is like closing the door on part of our lives.

Too often, men and women in the *third age* wait for a major turning point in their lives before confronting a decision on where to live. This may involve sickness, a death in the family or a dramatic decline in a city neighborhood that makes them feel unsafe. It can be loss of a job or, more likely, retirement. Whatever, moving is never easy.

Behind the difficulties and the trauma of moving stands a major fact of life: *where* we live determines to a large degreee *how* we live. It determines the friends we have or do not have, the people we see regularly, the activities we engage in, the facilities we have access to. By the *third age*, different criteria apply to the choice of housing — what kind and where. Local schools no longer matter; household space for children empties as they grow up and leave; traveling to work looms larger or may no longer be a consideration.

Meanwhile, career and job assume different aspects. The focus on getting ahead begins to shift toward getting more satisfaction from work, personal time and living in general. Unless economic pressures are acute, the shift is from making a living to making a life. With retirement, housing decisions often become imperative. As retirement counselor Curtis H. Moore of Rockford, Illinois, reports, people who turn up at his retirement classes are "scared." They arrive "absolutely blank." Among them are "heads of large firms and blue-collar workers." Retirement is a universal leveler.

Dr. Moore makes the valid point that there are "no pat answers except that a 10-year period is almost minimal if you want to do something about planning your finances, your housing, your leisure time."

Leo Baldwin, housing coordinator for the American Association of Retired Persons, warns that mistakes are most frequently made and options reduced when a housing decision is made during a crisis, such as an accident or ill health. "By then," he notes, "most of us do not have the time or the opportunity to hunt around and do the research that is needed."

Looking ahead is important for both practical and psychological reasons. It lays the groundwork for choices and helps to make the most suitable choices become reality. At retirement, housing choices involve:

• Moving to another community or another kind of housing.
  • Living with grown children.
  • Senior citizen housing.
  • Retirement communities.

Sometimes by changing jobs and/or careers, men and women in their 50s change their housing in anticipation of retiring. Sometimes, change follows emptying of the family nest. As grown children go off on their own, a smaller home or apartment is in order, or even possibly a move to the city from suburbia.

The pronounced trend is for older Americans to live on their own rather than with their grown children. This is not only the case with older couples, but with all older Americans. The number who live alone has increased dramatically, reflecting both the trend and the growing population over 65. During the decade of the 1970s the number of people 65 and over living alone increased by 48 percent — from 5.1 million to 7.5 million.

This does not mean loss of contact with grown children and relatives. Rather, it reflects the emphasis in our society on autonomy and independence. Living alone also reflects the differences between the generations in tastes, attitudes, values and approaches to life. Living under the same roof with grown children can and does work, but it requires degrees of compatibility and acceptance that are not easy to come by. So experts agree that it is generally better if parents do not move back with grown children, particularly when they have families. (Of course, there are many exceptions where this is working well.)

Moving itself involves choices on both type of housing and location. The answer centers on what is appropriate to a changing life situation and the future years. Whereas decisions on housing were made by putting children first during the *second age*, the focus shifts in the *third age*. Different criteria apply. Key questions to ask include:

Is there easy access to shopping either by walking or public transportation? Are there cultural and educational opportunities nearby? What about medical facilities? What is the climate like during all 12 months of the year? Is the housing near a metropolitan area where there is employment? There are two aspects to this latter question: being near an employment center makes resale of a house easier and also makes it more likely that work is available, if a *third age* man or woman still wants to do productive work. Going further, it is possible to research an area to see whether available work matches one's skills, experiences and interests.

An increasing number of older Americans have made the decision to move. They are called the "mobile elderly" by Dr. Charles F. Longino Jr., director of the Center for Social Research in Aging at the University of Miami. They largely account for the fourfold increase during the 1970s — compared with the 1960s — in men and women over 60 who moved from one state to another. Of those 1.7 million who moved, nearly half went to five states: Florida, California, Arizona, Texas and New Jersey. Florida was, by far, the most popular choice, having received more than one-fourth of all interstate migrants over 60 during the 1960s and 1970s. It has the largest proportion (17.3 percent) of elderly in the country, whereas California has the largest number of older Americans.

Two factors played a major role. Many Americans over 60 are more affluent than any previous generation their age. Many of them are World War II veterans who became accustomed to moving away to colleges and universities and then to moving with change of jobs. According to Dr. Longino: "These mobile elderly have more money, are better educated and are more comfortable about the idea of moving than any previous group of retirees in history."

There is both good and bad news for those who consider moving — and it all depends on who is talking and who is listening. Different people have different experiences. For some, moving south means fulfillment of a dream of sun and fun, of replacing the work-ethic with the play-ethic. They discover a new circle of friends and they escape the ravages of cold weather. For others, the life becomes boring and lonely, lacking in stimuli and in satisfying activities.

When a *Wall Street Journal* reporter visited Port Charlotte, Florida, he reported: "Keeping busy is the business of Port Charlotte." On one hand, he found retirees who said: "Want to keep busy? Retire" . . . "You're never bored." On the other hand, the coordinator of Charlotte County's adult and community education program, said: "Our battle is loneliness. A lot of people dream about paradise. They sell their homes and move here. After the drapes are up and the carpets are down, the paradise can turn into a living hell if they don't find something to do."

At Tampa's University of South Florida, anthropologist Maria Vesperi commented that people act too hastily in moving south. "They don't look carefully enough at options," she said. "They turn 65, and they come down here because they think it's the thing to do. They make snap judgments about buying, and then they're stuck. The difference in prices is just enough to make it very hard to go back. Many have been constrained by finances — or just plain embarrassment. You tell people, 'We're moving to Florida.' You really can't go back without losing a lot of pride."

For anyone planning to move from one part of the country to another, a gradual transition is recommended by the experts. They suggest several extended visits during different seasons of the year before making a final decision. A two-step approach is also proposed: adjusting first to retirement and then moving a year or more later.

Actually, most men and women in the *third age* stay put. Seventy percent of those age 65 and over will probably occupy their present homes for the rest of their lives, according to studies by the American Association of Retired Persons. Only four percent are migrating to other states. A similar survey in 1980 by the University of Connecticut confirms the desire to stay put. Of those 60 and older, 85 percent said they want to remain in their homes if it can be worked out.

For homeowners, a house is their main financial equity. It is also psychologically important. In America, owning your own home has traditionally meant, "We've made it!" Moving out of a house after many years means facing the fact that things have changed. Sometimes, the decision is made to move to a smaller, more manageable and more economical house. A house bought for a family of five or six is much more than two people need and a heavy financial burden, particularly in a time of high energy costs and rising taxes. A house, as well, involves built-in extra costs, particulary the need for a car.

The current location may no longer be an advantage as not only grown children move away but so do friends. Staying in the same house could mean growing isolation and extra time and effort to stay involved and active. An assessment of the situation depends on the particular area and the involvements that have developed and are still available. Clearly, it doesn't make sense to maintain a "Christmas house" where once or twice a year family members reunite for the holidays while otherwise most of the rooms are empty and unused. Certainly, when such a home means increasing isolation and shrinking boundaries for living and seeing people, then it is time to reconsider.

Early in the *third age*, men and women are urged by financial experts to take stock of their retirement income. The mid-40s are a sensible time to begin such planning or at least 10 to 15 years before retirement. This involves a close look at personal resources, including Social Security payments, pensions, annuities, and individual retirement accounts.

While most people resist the idea of creating a budget, planning without hard numbers is likely to be wishful thinking. Basically, this involves figuring out pre-retirement expenses and estimating retirement expenses in the following categories beginning with housing:

- ☐ Rent/Mortgage payments
- ☐ Food
- ☐ Clothing
- ☐ Amusement, hobbies
- ☐ Health care
- ☐ Automobile, gas, repair
- ☐ Telephone, utilities
- ☐ House repair
- ☐ Furniture, other household items
- ☐ Personal items
- ☐ Working expenses
- ☐ Insurance: house/life/car
- ☐ Income taxes: federal/state/local
- ☐ Property taxes
- ☐ Other items

With adjustments for inflation, projected expenses can be compared with expected retirement income. There are different estimates of what is needed. While studies show that a retired couple can live comfortably on less than they needed before retirement, the difference may not be as great as assumed for a comfortable life with some luxuries. Estimates range from as low as 55 percent of pre-retirement income to as high as 80 percent, depending on scale of living.

The local office of the Social Security Administration is a starting place for information, including publications such as: *Thinking About Retiring?, Your Social Security, Your Social Security Rights and Responsibilities.* City and state agencies provide information as do banks and organizations. (See appendix for details on sources of information and assistance.)

Fortunately, various solutions are emerging to help retired people meet the expenses of keeping their own home. Some homeowners are renting space, others are creating accessory apartments. Communities are reducing property taxes for older homeowners and various states are setting up agencies to assist in home-sharing arrangements. In addition, reverse-equity mortgages are providing a fixed monthly income to anyone with a debt-free home, with the amount paid out, plus interest, deducted from eventual sale price of the house.

In striking a balance between autonomy and security, senior citizen housing and retirement communities are proving the answer for many men and women. But not without criticism from those who decry the isolation and the symbolic segregation. That is a limited view which doesn't take into account individual differences. For many who have made the choice special housing offers a wonderful opportunity to establish a network of personal relationships.

Senior citizen housing offers conveniences and facilities geared to older residents, while retirement communities usually provide individual homes for a younger group of residents who are relatively affluent. Before getting involved, it makes sense to examine the setup carefully and to check on the sponsorship.

Each couple, each person needs to make an individual decision after examining the options. While retirement communities have been dismissed by some critics as Disneylands for older Americans, they offer distinct benefits: freedom from upkeep, friends and neighbors with common interests, and organized activities.

Two researchers, Gordon L. Bultena and Vivian Wood, have drawn a positive picture of retirement communities in describing the "prodigious efforts" of community developers "to legitimize a leisure role for retirees." They report that three out of four people living in retirement communities are "very satisified" with their lives compared with 57 percent of retirees outside retirement communities.

Innovations are also appearing in housing opportunities. These include small, self-contained houses designed for installation in the backyards of existing single-family homes, cooperatively run houses, and group homes that hire a staff to operate them. In one of the most creative housing moves, colleges are turning unused dormitories into apartments for mature men and women.

At Nazareth College near Kalamazoo, Michigan, men and women from 60 to 92 moved into a dormitory whose space was converted into 75 one-bedroom apartments. The generations are mixing wonderfully. Student reactions included: "It's kind of like having surrogate grandparents". . . . "You can gain insight into the future because they've lived through the past." The men and women can take courses tuition-free at the college and enjoy campus life, including cultural activities. One husband reported that he and his wife make a point of auditing one course each semester. "It's got our brains stirring again," he said. "They forced me to work. I hadn't been inside a classroom since 1938."

Regardless of housing decision, hospitality needs to be a common thread. A house or apartment without hospitality is not a home. It does not have the spirit of sharing that enlivens and enriches our lives. This applies to individuals living alone or couples. Openness to others is expressed by an open-door approach that welcomes other people of all ages and background. Opportunities for hospitality make one choice of housing much more attractive than another.

Parish and neighborhood are natural settings for a sense of community and belonging. A parish which has togetherness and outreach is a good place to stay in or move to. It is a natural setting for the generations to contribute to each other and for older parishioners to provide the social memory and glue for the people living there.

Neighborhoods, like people, have personalities. Some are lively and interesting, a joy to be in contact with. Others are reserved, uninviting and uninteresting. Just as we choose our friends so should we choose our neighborhoods and communities during the *third age*. The enemy is inertia, the ally is conscious choice.

Whether a married couple or an individual, the two common reasons for moving are to live near children and to move to a warm climate. In either case, the move involves going to another community with a determination to create a new social network. Problems lie in wait for couples who move and depend only on each other or their grown children for social contacts.

Just as older parents can become too dependent on their grown children, so too can grown children interfere with the autonomy of their parents. In growing up, children complain about parents not letting them be independent; in later years, grown children can be guilty of similar pressures directed toward their own parents.

For those grown children who pay too little attention to their parents, there are others who act out of guilt and become overly intrusive in the lives of their parents. Joel and Lois Davitz, who studied the behavior of grown children toward their parents, warn: "Treating an elderly parent as helpless can be psychologically devastating." Going to the other extreme of expecting too much is also a problem. Asking too much is as undesirable as asking too little.

Behind a discussion of where to live, a new reality is emerging for men and women in the *third age*. As already mentioned, we are moving toward family-like structures that expand the notion of family. Men and women in the *third age* are discovering and developing sets of relationships beyond the traditional family. These extra-family relationships are providing emotional support. Freely chosen networks of friends are becoming increasingly important.

There are many examples as people discover each other in their neighborhoods, parish and community. It happens both formally in organizations and groups and informally. Neighbors form the habit of looking in on each other and helping each other. Fellow parishioners at daily Mass notice if someone is missing and maintain a circle of mutual help.

A number of significant forces are at work. Families are spread all over the country due to the mobility of American society. Also, now four generations are often involved and family complications are evident in the number of divorces, separations and remarriages that exist. Just as the family becomes more spread out, the traditional family is no longer a tight little enclosure.

A new greening of society is taking place where family means not only those related by blood. In everyday terms, "family" is coming to include those with whom we are in close and regular contact, those with a shared sense of mutual responsibility and caring. This is consistent with the notion of the Gospel message that we are all brothers and sisters by reason of a life in Jesus Christ. We can form such common bonds wherever we live.

SEVEN

Graying of the Parish

FOR OLDER Catholics in particular, religion is where their parish is — the focal point for religious identity, service and ministry. To paraphrase a Kennedyism — Catholics in the *third age* are not only asking what the parish can do for them, they are asking what they can do for the parish. Given the trends in the Catholic population and the sources of greatest support for the Catholic Church, older Catholics are more important than ever in the life of the parish.

In the Catholic parish, from one-fourth to two-fifths of its parishioners are over 50, particularly in the cities. This means that the parish no longer can afford to concentrate on the young at the expense of the rest of its parishioners. The graying of the parish presents an unprecedented challenge to the Church at its grass roots — in the geographical unit where people connect with their religious commitment.

As Vatican Council II reaffirmed so emphatically: "Because it is impossible for the bishop always and everywhere to preside over the whole flock in his church, he cannot do other than establish lesser groupings of the faithful. Among these, parishes set up locally under a pastor who takes the place of the bishop are the most important, for in a certain way they represent the visible Church as it is established throughout the world."

The parish is a totality, a community of believers joined in their faith and commitment. It is not a religious service station where members come for religious refueling and occasional repairs. It is an ongoing expression of what it means to believe and act out beliefs. Service — as well as worship — is a hallmark of such a community.

The parish, however, is not one-directional in terms of who is providing services and who is receiving them. Particularly since Vatican Council II, the parish is characterized more and more by involvement. It is not only the clergy serving the faithful and it is not only a youth-centered geographical entity. It is clergy and laity, single and married, young and old working together to give witness by giving of themselves.

The parish is a place where its members do important things together. They praise God together. They learn together and it should be a place where they laugh together and where they wipe away tears together. Also, it is a place where people are called forth in the original meaning of the Greek word, *ecclesia* (assembly), meaning the coming together of religious believers.

The concept of stewardship is crucial to the relationship of all Catholics with their individual parishes. *Third age* Catholics stand out in this regard. For the most part, they are ready, willing and able to go far beyond the notion of what they can receive from the parish. They have much to give and are giving much.

Older Catholics personify the elements of stewardship: time, talent, treasure and tenacity. They have more time to commit, particularly as the task of raising children is behind them and the demands of job and career lessen. They have the talent, based on experience, know-how and prolonged activity. While some face financial pressures, others carry lessened financial burdens, particularly older Catholics who are still working.

Tenacity or perseverance deserves a special word. Older Catholics, who have endured difficulties, setbacks, and the vicissitudes of life, have demonstrated the fortitude to endure and to stick by their faith. They have continued on and they still continue as significant witnesses to the Gospel and to their faith.

In every parish, the witness of older Catholics is evident. They fill the front pews in early morning Masses. They attend novenas, retreats and special celebrations. They are seen visiting the church and praying. They are a backbone of the parish at worship and increasingly important to both service and ministry.

The authoritative 1982 Gallup report, *Religion in America,* documents the importance of *third age* men and women to church life (*Religion in America 1982,* published by the Princeton [N.J.] Religion Research Center). While the percentages encompass all Americans, it is reasonable to view the data as a reliable indication of Catholic attitudes in particular. Each set of figures shows that older Americans are the most involved and committed to religion of any age group. The overwhelming majority of those 50 and older pray (92 percent); believe God loves them (94 percent); try to put religious beliefs into practice (87 percent), and regard religion as the most important influence in life (79 percent).

Among those 50 and older who are church members, more than eight out of 10 give their own clergymen an "A" or "B" rating. Half of those 50 and over give clergymen an "A" rating compared with 31 percent of those under 30. In rating themselves on a scale of one to 10 for leading a Christian life, 59 percent of those 50 or older rate themselves at eight, nine, or 10 compared with 45 percent of those 30 to 49 and 29 percent of those under 30. Almost 70 percent of those 65 or over rate themselves at eight, nine, or 10. Moreover, more than half of those 50 or over give most of their friends such a rating — notably higher than any other age group. Finally, 84 percent of Americans over 50 report that they would welcome a greater role for religious beliefs in people's lives.

Within the Catholic Church, *third age* men and women can offer a special example in the way they accept change in parish and community life as they deal with change in their own lives. When *third age* Catholics stand out as fortified by their faith, when they find solace and direction in the Gospel message, when they give witness to the meaning they find in life, then they render their faith believable to others, particularly to younger people.

The Gospel provides examples of such witness in Simeon and Anna, the only two examples where age is mentioned in the Gospel. Each represents steadfastness, perseverance and a personification of tenacity. Anna, a widow who had watched and waited for many years, was rewarded with the gift of seeing the Messiah brought to the temple. So also with Simeon, who took the Lord into his arms and uttered those poignant words: "Now, Lord, you have kept your promise, and you may let your servant go in peace. With my own eyes I have seen your salvation . . ." (Luke 2:29-30).

There is no mistaking the widespread acceptance among older Catholics of new opportunities to participate and give witness. Based on nationwide experience and observation, it is clear that they are responding fully and completely to Church renewal. They welcome opportunities to participate. In fact, the most dramatic examples of such participation are to be found in homes for the aged. To join in such religious services is to feel the full force of perseverance in faith and participatory worship among older Catholics.

A summary of the responses at St. Peter Manor for the Aged in Memphis, Tennessee, is representative. Father Joseph Paolozzi, the chaplain, described elderly residents as "very pleased with the changes in the Church." They view the changes as "a challenge which excites them and in the end gives them a church from which they can get more and participate in more." He cited, in particular, acceptance of face-to-face confession, lay lectors, the sign of peace and Prayers of the Faithful requests.

"Like people of all ages," he added, "they were hesitant until we explained the reason for these innovations. Now, after the changes have been thoroughly explained, they are very popular aspects of their worship." Rather than an abrupt break with the past, a link is maintained with pre-conciliar devotions: "We update their devotions and we sing some of the old hymns and we use updated versions of some old prayer forms. This is perfectly in line with Council teaching and yet it adds a touch of the past. . . . . You must be careful not to disregard those old devotions by saying they have no value. What you must do is incorporate them into the Church in a whole new way of bringing people together and get away from the idea of having a prayer service just to have a prayer service."

At the Center on Pre-Retirement and Aging at The Catholic University of America, its acting director, Michael Creedon, reports that the relationship of older Catholics with their Church is continuously improving. He finds a new balance emerging that makes older Catholics feel at home:

"Today, with experimentation over, the Church is having a renewed appreciation of some of the old things, such as certain old hymns, choral music and other devotional forms. There was a time when all you had were guitar Masses, and now even that is tapering off. You are seeing a return to balance; more traditional forms of worship are being recognized more and more.''

Rather than a rejection or watering-down of Vatican II changes, he describes the current trend as a ''tapering off of the change-for-change-sake'' mentality. This is accompanied by greater appreciation of ''the positive values of past Church traditions and prayers and devotional forms.''

For their part, *third age* Catholics in parishes throughout the country are demonstrating their support for liturgical changes. Actually, younger and older Catholics are the most responsive; most resistance to change has come from middle-aged Catholics. Neal Parent of the adult education office of the U.S. Catholic Conference reports that older Catholics are ''excited and spurred on'' by opportunities for more participation. Charlotte Mahoney of the office of domestic development of the U.S. Catholic Conference agrees, noting that older Catholics ''are like the young people in adapting well to Church renewal.''

The phenomenon is evident in parishes throughout the country. Older Catholics regularly celebrate the liturgy and participate in the community that is created. Parishioners notice who is there for the service and who is missing. They greet each other and ask about those who are not there. To them the parish church is not a headquarters for bingo and outings or fairs. It is the headquarters for the very stuff of life, for religious nourishment and expression of commitment to their faith.

Without fanfare and without widespread attention, the life of the parish is also being conducted on the level of loving care for those in need, particularly the frail of all ages. Older Catholics are giving as well as receiving such care. The dimensions of such care are not fully known and that, as a matter of fact, is why the Third Age Center at Fordham University has undertaken a nationwide study of care-giving techniques in 18,000 U.S. parishes.

The care ranges from an informal system of phone checks to ongoing care of the frail. Parishes are acting as intermediaries, bringing together care-givers of all kinds and people who need care. On both sides of the equation, older Catholics predominate. Specifically, here are examples of the care-giving:

Shopping for the home-bound;

Phoning every day to make sure that elderly men and women are all right;

Regular visiting to make certain needs are taken care of;

Home nursing care.

In the borough of Queens in New York City, for example, on any given day in 20 different parishes people who have the time and people who have needs are put in contact — with the parish as intermediary. This is clearly a growing trend, especially in American cities where alienation and isolation threaten urban parishioners.

Specifically, parishes can do the following:

Establish a "senior adoption" program in which families adopt an elderly person whom they will visit regularly, call on the phone, and with whom they will share birthday and holiday celebrations and occasional family dinners.

Publish a directory for parish families with information about county, state, federal programs of assistance and other services for elderly persons. Include information on parish programs and services for the elderly, as well as opportunities in the parish for elderly persons to provide leadership and services.

Convert an unused parish building into low-cost housing for senior citizens. Contact public housing agencies for information and assistance.

While traditional concern for the frail, the sick and the lonely will always elicit a response from the Church, the challenge reaches beyond the realm of charitable service. Increasing attention must be paid to older adults who want to make meaningful contributions to the Church's mission. While ministry to and of older adults may take place in many places and under many circumstances, the parish is the most significant place of all.

Encouragement of older persons to be involved in ministry must first be accompanied by a self-examination on the part of everyone involved in the parish. Are the elderly made to feel that they are a vital part of the Christian community so that their talents and gifts — indeed their age — are used for the enrichment of the Church? Are serious efforts being made by local congregations to offer opportunities for ministry among older adults, or are elderly people viewed primarily as recipients of charitable services?

In an example of the way in which the time and talents of older Catholics are tapped, a parish in Albany, New York, turned to its Golden Age Club for confirmation sponsors. Some of the youngsters did not have adult sponsors and so the Golden Agers became surrogate sponsors. They became involved in the preparations, including the instructions, and their enthusiasm became infectious.

When other members of the Golden Age Club heard about what was happening and learned about the textbooks and the instruction, they became curious. They became interested in catching up on their own religious education. They were saying, "Hey, look at the new textbooks. . . . We never had anything like this. . . . We don't understand all this new material. . . . Why can't we have instructions too?" Special classes were then set up — a powerful example of the ripple effect from greater involvement in the life of the parish.

All over the country, parishes are challenged to respond to the needs, wants and demands of older parishioners who want to learn more about their faith. The demand for Scripture study stands out as older Catholics demonstrate renewed interest in the Word of God. They want to read Scriptures, discuss what they read and study with a knowledgeable guide. In one parish, a two-hour Scripture study group met once a week during Lent after a 9 o'clock weekday Mass. It was educational and prayerful. The response was enthusiastic.

There is a powerful lesson here: teaching in the parish is not limited to the young. Teaching and learning is a parish-wide process that includes clergy as well as laity. A fundamental principle is involved; it is built on the need for the preacher to learn from those he preaches to. This means listening to *third age* people, their needs, hopes, aspirations, their anxieties and their collective wisdom. Any clergyman who has reached out in this way testifies to his own enrichment and increased effectiveness.

Parishes ought to establish groups of *third age* Catholics so that individual parishioners can come together and reflect on their experiences. They need the opportunity to discuss what it means to be in the *third age* as an individual and as a Catholic. They want to reflect on the meaning of their current stage of life in the light of the Gospel message. They can revel in the value and benefit of shared faith as they share what they know, feel and believe.

Even the parish is too large. Parishioners need small groups that come together regularly to give witness and to share themselves as well as their faith. Where this is introduced — as in the Archdiocese of Newark, New Jersey — the response speaks to the need and to the readiness to participate.

In the area of ministry, the fruits of personal participation are personified by Eucharistic ministers. They are going to homebound parishioners and bringing to them the Bread of Life in many ways. At Mass, these ministers are coming forward to receive a single host to bring to parishioners who cannot get out. It results in deeply enriched encounters that demonstrate the unity of the parish community.

Often, the Eucharistic minister brings the entire family after Mass. Husband, wife and children visit the elderly parishioner and bring human contact along with the Eucharist. The glow of family life encompasses the homebound person and there is no doubt the givers receive as much as the recipients. It is a powerful example for the young when Christian witness unfolds in deed rather than preachment. The children in such families don't need to be told that their parents believe and that their faith makes a difference in their lives.

While a minority of older Catholics are homebound, the large majority represent an enormous resource for ministry. The parish has every right to call upon *third age* Catholics, who for their part are often only waiting to be asked. Many already are taking the initiative in service and ministry and many more are ready to join in.

All over the country, in one parish after another, *third age* Catholics are rediscovering involvement. Typical of their reactions is the remark heard time and again in almost the same words: "I just regret that I didn't have this opportunity to participate when I was younger."

It is a statement that reflects changes in the Church as well as changes in their own lives and attitudes. They are in the *third age* of life, a time of opening up to others, as well as themselves, a time of awareness and of service. It is a time for coming to terms with their faith in the concrete — in the parish as center of religious identity, service and ministry.

EIGHT

Working for Justice

OLDER Americans are at a new threshold in making their voices heard in state and federal governments. Besides standing up for their legitimate self-interest, it is important that they go beyond special pleading and work for a just society that balances everyone's interests and needs. For Catholics in particular, this means taking into account the prime cardinal virtue of justice so that the future as well as the present is served and so that the benefits and the sacrifices of U.S. society are distributed fairly. Both grandchildren and grandparents — as well as working generations in-between — have legitimate demands that bear consideration.

The crisis in financing Social Security dramatized the role of government in all our lives and also raised the threat of creating conflicts between the generations as taxes on the employed were weighed against payments to the retired. However, this issue, like others that older Americans need to address, is not limited to one age group. Christian sensibility demands that everyone be his or her neighbor's keeper. Just as society cannot neglect the older generation, neither can the older generation ignore the needs, problems and interests of younger generations. Otherwise, the pessimists will find their warning coming true: a young-against-old revolution.

The forceful leader of the militant Gray Panthers, 77-year-old Margaret Kuhn, did not hesitate to warn in discussing the controversy over Social Security: "Many of the old people are self-centered and pleading for themselves. We're saying we're all in it together. . . (and that) the confusion and fear have got to be eliminated."

The United States is in the midst of a major adjustment to the graying of its population and the emergence of an increasing proportion of people in the *third age* of life. In that stage — occurring sometime around the age of 50 — families have been raised and individuals have become established in job, career and community. Others in the U.S. population are in the *first age* (growing up and getting an education) and in the *second age* (building a career and raising a family). All ages need to be served.

At the federal level, government has led the way in responding to the changes in U.S. society involving 26 million Americans over 65 (in 1983) and increasing numbers of *third age* Americans who are retiring early. The U.S. Bureau of Labor statistics reports that only 18 percent of men 65 and older were working in 1982, compared with 48 percent in 1947. Among men 55 to 64, about 70 percent worked in 1982, compared with 87 percent in 1950.

In 1983, no less than 27 percent of the federal budget, including defense, was devoted to the needs of older Americans. This includes a wide range of benefits and programs: Social Security, Medicare, Medicaid, Veterans Administration, Civil Service retirement, housing and nutritional programs, and Senior Citizen work programs plus other programs not geared to age, but which benefit large numbers of older Americans.

Far-reaching government involvement with the needs of older Americans is nothing short of revolutionary as that involvement has accelerated since the Social Security Act was signed into law. The timetable speaks for itself:

1935 — Social Security Act signed;

1939 — Benefits added for dependents and survivors;

1950-1960 — Social Security coverage added for domestic workers, federal employees not covered by the federal retirement program, members of the armed forces and the self-employed;

1965 — Hospital insurance under Medicare added to the Social Security system;

1967 — Ministers and members of religious orders not under vows of poverty added to Social Security;

1972 — Social Security benefits indexed to the inflation rate.

Today, 92 percent of Americans over 65 receive Social Security benefits compared with only 60 percent in 1960. Social Security represents the largest single source of income for older Americans, providing 38 percent of their total income. Next come earnings from employment, 23 percent; followed by income from assets, 19 percent. Private and government pensions each provide seven percent. Only two percent comes from public assistance, with the remaining four percent from other sources.

The generosity in the system is measured by the return on Social Security payments that were made by wage earners. Someone who retired in 1980 paid $24,206 and could be expected to collect $125,125. Today, for every Social Security retiree, there are 3.2 wage earners supporting him or her. Meanwhile, as the average family income dropped by a little under one percent between 1970 and 1981, average annual income for those 65 and over increased almost 13 percent. Average monthly Social Security benefits for retired persons increased by 40 percent.

In addition, the federal government has provided a variety of tax benefits for older Americans — special income tax deductions, property tax relief, forgiveness of capital gains tax in sale of a home after age 55. To further protect older Americans, the federal government has taken aggressive steps against age discrimination, leading the way in eliminating mandatory retirement at age 65.

These facts add up to a significant point: the United States government has a tremendous commitment to its older citizens. It is a commitment that has grown tremendously in recent decades and that commitment transcends party affiliations. It is nothing less than a national consensus.

All this has come under the heading of justice rather than charity, which is in tune with the point made by Vatican Council II: "The demands of justice should be first satisfied, lest the giving of what is due in justice be represented as the offering of a charitable gift."

Meanwhile, older Americans have developed a sense of group consciousness that is clearly in the tradition of other power movements of recent decades: black power, student power, women's power. Now gray power has come to the fore. No less than 22 national organizations represent the interests of older Americans. The largest, the American Association of Retired Persons, has 14 million members and is a powerful lobby with a massive telephone network.

Other groups range from the National Council of Senior Citizens with four million members to the Gray Panthers with 60,000 members. Eighty-two-year-old Claude Pepper — the powerful Congressman known as "Mr. Aging" — was named to head the Senior PAC, a political-action committee. In addition, Save Our Security (SOS) was formed as an umbrella coalition of 141 seniors' organizations, labor unions, churches, and other groups dedicated to defending the Social Security system.

With power comes responsibility, including the responsibility to avoid setting groups of Americans at odds with each other. This danger already surfaced in the controversy over Social Security. A phrase such as "institutionalized pick-pocketing" of the young was used to describe Social Security by the head of Strategic Economic Decisions in California, Horace W. Brock. In an opinion column for *Newsweek* magazine, a professor of economics, Walter E. Williams, depicted Social Security as "at once a bad deal, a lie and a national obstruction." Weigh such remarks against the statement of Representative Pepper and the bitter seeds of conflict are evident: "Social Security is the lifeblood of millions. If somebody were tinkering with your only means of survival, wouldn't you be sensitive about it?"

For groups concerned with the problems of older Americans and for individual Americans in the *third age*, a single-issue outlook serves neither them nor their society and can even cast a shadow over the future. This does not mean that older Americans should retreat from their legitimate demand for financial and medical protection. It certainly does not mean forgetting the 20 percent or more of those Americans over 65 who live in precarious straits around the government's poverty-line income of $4,400 a year.

Moreover, older women as a group face economic hardships stemming from the fact that they have longer life spans and lower retirement income than men. In fact, 90 percent of women in private industry retire with no pensions. One-third of elderly women depend on Social Security for 90 percent or more of their income, and the amount they receive is consistently lower than the amount paid to men. In 1982, the average monthly Social Security benefit paid to adult women was $308 compared with $430 paid to men. A George Washington University study made the point that "by every economic measure, women are more deprived in their later years than are men."

Margaret Kuhn of the Gray Panthers describes the situation forcefully: "The prospects for retirement [by women] are not pleasant. In our present Social Security system, benefits are calculated on what you have paid in. If you've never had decent jobs, if your employment record is spotty or interrupted, you're going to get a relatively lower Social Security benefit. Linked to that is the fact that women are survivors, outliving men anywhere from eight to 13 years. It's desperately needed for women — if they can accept this — that they should continue to be gainfully and usefully employed." Or as Massachusetts Congressman Barney Frank has stated: "The major error we have to correct in the retirement system is the discrimination against housewives and mothers."

For those Americans whose only income is from Social Security, the possibility of cutbacks in benefits is a clear and present danger. During the 1982-1983 controversy over Social Security, Lou Glasse, director of the New York State Department on Aging, warned of the consequences of cutting back on supplemental security income, Medicare, Medicaid, food stamps, energy assistance, meals and other programs. Mr. Glasse said bluntly: "It can't help but cause tragedy for many elderly persons." In California, the director of the Commission on Aging, John Riggle, reported that "the outlook is pretty grim." In Colorado, the director of the Department on Aging, William Hanna, raised the bitter prospect "of having to determine which of the elderly poor are most needy."

At the same time that the legitimate cry of justice

for the have-nots (of all ages) demands attention, the picture of older Americans must not be blurred. Most of them are better off than their counterparts of 10 or 20 years ago. Older Americans had an average household income of $12,628 in 1983, or 60 percent of the average U.S. household income. By comparison, in 1970 older Americans had an average income that was only 48 percent of the national average. Moreover, 70 percent of older Americans own their own homes and 80 percent of them have paid off their mortgages.

This balanced economic picture is a basis for sorting out demands made upon the government. In the first place, there is the legitimate struggle to support Social Security, Medicare, Medicaid and other age-related government programs. But that cannot constitute the be-all and end-all of involvement in public issues for older Americans. They belong in the overall fight against poverty, disease and social neglect as it affects *all* Americans. That is both sound Americanism and sound Christianity.

From the Christian perspective, involvement in public issues cannot be properly limited to a single issue to the exclusion of other issues and other considerations. What needs to be said to older Americans is this: "Remember what the government has done and is doing for you. By all means, demand your rights and campaign for the needs of older Americans. But don't stop there. You can't ignore the crisis of a federal budget deficit that endangers the entire society. You can't close your eyes to environmental problems, to acid rain, to dumping of hazardous waste."

Fortunately, older Americans constitute a receptive audience for this message. This is evident to anyone who travels around the country talking to groups of older Americans and carrying on discussions with them. As *The Wall Street Journal* reported in discussing a nationwide poll of senior citizens by the Louis Harris Organization: "Most see themselves as resilient survivors who want to keep making significant contributions to the mainstream of American life."

Individually, older Americans are a reservoir of social and historical memory. They are witnesses to what it was like when so many of the social and economic gains that now are taken for granted were never there. They lived through times — recent times that are easily forgotten — when racism was prevalent; as was second-class status for women; when unemployment benefits and health insurance were not available as a safety net. They have experienced social progress and they can give witness to what was not and what is now. Just as older people are the cement in family life, they are the cement in community life.

In the *third age* of life, the Beatitudes are as relevant as ever and they certainly do not set a retirement age when Christians can stop being merciful, stop being peacemakers, stop humgering and thirsting for holiness. Being involved in the needs of others and responsive to the problems in society involve fundamental Gospel values. In that sense, a Christian never retires and never asks only of government: what can you do for me?

NINE

Growing in Holiness

FOR CATHOLICS committed to religious growth, the mature years can become the best of spiritual times, offering the greatest opportunities to grow in belief, faith and holiness. Maturity is harvesttime for seeds of personal holiness planted in youth and adulthood. It is the stage of life when time, experience and situation provide fertile ground for cultivating our relationship with God.

Despite the saccharine treatment it has received from popularized versions, holiness is not Ingrid Bergman in a nun's costume or Barry Fitzgerald and Bing Crosby in Roman collars. It is a powerful and sustaining process of turning toward the Lord of Creation.

Holiness is the daily effort to deepen our awareness of God's presence and the struggle to respond to the Lord's promptings on how we should lead our lives. It involves the conscious and constant process of trying to penetrate the mystery of God and God's relationship with people. It is acting on the Lord's promptings in what we say, how we feel and what we do. It is life in the spiritually active tense.

The more mature we are the better equipped we are to develop holiness in this demanding and fulfilling sense. The older we get, the further we can move forward from childhood and adolescence in the *first age* of life when growing up and establishing personal identity are predominant and distracting. In the *second age* of life, when making a living and meeting family responsibilities dominate adult years, the demands from the outside make it difficult to meet the needs from inside. Life then is more reaction than reflection, more application than analysis and more outward than inward.

By contrast, the *third age* dawns with new opportunities. It is the period of life when the responsibilities of parenting are over and children are on their own. It is the period when an individual man or woman is established in job, career, community and church. Goals that have been met are taken for granted and adjustments are made for those unrealized goals. Dreams of the past have given way to realities of the present, and the stage is set for new goals, including spiritual growth.

Greater freedom and more time are the circumstances, greater maturity — coming from greater knowledge, experience and understanding — is the means. At about age 50, life has presented itself with its ups and downs and, having endured both, each individual has the chance for greater perspective. The growing awareness of time passing adds a note of urgency to the process of distinguishing what really counts from what hardly matters.

For religious persons, there is only one direction to look in order to focus on what really matters in life. It is to God. Less distracted, more attuned to fundamentals, *third age* Catholics are less likely to look elsewhere, more receptive and better prepared to engage the religious dimension of their lives. Here a realistic point needs to be made: *growing older does not make people more religious.* How religious people are reflects how religious they have been all their lives. The observation that older people are more religious than younger people results from the fact that these same people were more religious when younger. The quest for holiness that takes place in earlier years carries forward — as does indifference. Chance, of course, occurs, but it is more exception than rule.

On the other hand, the *third age* brings men and women closer to the serious questions of life. Death comes as a reminder whether it be death in the family or death among friends. It is a reminder of personal mortality and of the fragility of passing fancies. It shows up distractions for what they are — escape from the fullness of life's mysteries. For the Christian, there is loss in order to celebrate resurrection and the mystery of redemption.

Here, it needs to be emphasized that holiness is not a checklist of *do's* and *don'ts*, rules and regulations, orders and obligations that add up to a certificate of sanctification. Holiness is not rote behavior. It is the fruit of an all-encompassing outlook in terms of God and the transcendent.

For many *third age* people, an adjustment is necessary with regard to external religious norms as the be-all and end-all of holiness. Of course, the norms are still there for Catholics: the Ten Commandments and the Laws of the Church. However they are not meant to create holiness out of conformity and obedience. They provide a common point of reference as well as a supporting framework.

Each individual must cultivate his or her personal uniqueness. Each must work out holiness in a distinct way as a glorious line of saints have demonstrated through the ages. For St. Therese of Lisieux it was the contemplative life, for Joan of Arc the heroic. For Francis of Assisi it was contemplation in the midst of nature, for Ignatius Loyola it was founding a powerful religious order. Each demonstrated that holiness has a historical setting as well as a deeply personal structure.

In our time, Thomas Merton's journey toward holiness demonstrated what he meant in stating that "our life . . . provokes us with the evidence that it must have meaning," though part of the meaning escapes us. "Yet our purpose in life is to discover this meaning, and live according to it." In his life of conversion and of Trappist contemplation, he sought that meaning and learned to live according to it. It is noteworthy that later in life he found that he also had to be involved in the problems of his times — racism, war, injustice — or otherwise he would be a "guilty bystander."

Holiness is saying to oneself, "In the time remaining to me, how am I to use my talents in pursuing the Kingdom of God and immersing myself in the process of becoming ever more deeply involved in reflecting on and responding to the presence of God?"

Each individual has a unique gift to provide, each has the task of discerning that gift and of overcoming inertia and indifference. The unexamined spiritual life is the underdeveloped spiritual life. The examined life creates awareness of what each of us has in talents, gifts, experience and opportunity. The answers are not ready-made and they are partial, but they are our own.

The process begins, endures and ends in turning toward God. The dimensions of self-examination and self-awareness are necessary parts of the introspection that is involved. It is necessary to take account of the forces that have an impact on each of us: physiological, psychological, social, economic. These differ with each age and each individual and these differences must be taken into account as the Christian goes further than these natural, humanistic considerations. The Christian lives and breathes in awareness of the transcendental dimension of the living, responsive God.

Here, the question of holiness touches on the fundamental mystery of Christianity: how is each individual free in terms of the presence of God? The Christian asks: How am I free and not free? What is this reality created by interaction with God, a reality that would not occur naturally?

In the examples of the saints, this involves an "emptying out" and opening up to the Lord. For *third age* Catholics most involved in the process of spiritual discernment, this can mean the experience of the dark night of the soul. It is the point at which the Christian says, "Lord, help me in my confusion." It is then that natural supports seem to give way and the Lord moves in His mysterious and fulfilling ways. What emerges is the Christian's realization that God *does* move in the lives of people.

Prayer is basic to this process. It acknowledges God as the focal point. It is the experience of a personal God who speaks to us in a multitude of modes. He speaks not only through human voices in Scripture; He also speaks to us in signs, in sounds, in the beauty and symphony of nature, in the joy of loving and being loved. We as Christians make the connections between what we experience and how we experience it with God.

Besides internal, personalized prayer, there is the external dimension, that is the sharing with others, whether it is family prayer, the prayer of the faithful at Mass, the sharing in the charismatic movement. In the home — between husband and wife — there is the opportunity for a simple, straightforward prayer built into the fabric of the day. It can arise as a short, sweet prelude to a meal together in terms of the moment and the circumstances. Here, prayer is externalized, but still personalized.

Structured prayer arises out of creative forms of praying that were effective at different times in the history of the Church. These forms become incorporated into the life of the faithful and become part of the liturgy to be shared by everyone. In group sharing, prayer must also have a personal, internal dimension in order to be truly meaningful, though it is stylized and structured.

For priests, reading the Breviary is an example of structured, stylized prayer. For that very reason, some priests have faulted this as rote religion, but they are overlooking a crucial point. Such reading sets the stage for personal prayer and, indeed, to give up reading the Breviary is to risk drifting away from prayer. The very structure points the individual in the direction of personal prayer.

As a phenomenon in the life of Christians, prayer arises both reactively and creatively. It is reactive in response to circumstances and crisis as Christians turn to God for support and sustenance in the face of trouble, pain, suffering, need. There is also prayer that arises spontaneously out of deep conviction and the desire to acknowledge the wondrous ways of the Lord and His universe.

Prayer enables us to confront our own weakness and in that confrontation to find strength. It is a paradox: seeing ourselves as weak and yet finding strength. It is the opposite of the escapism that is so prevalent as people rush toward drugs, alcohol, entertainment, sports, television and busy-ness. Instead of running toward our true selves, we are tempted by the world of *having* and *doing* to run away. Prayer that recognizes the slender thread by which life hangs and its very contingency reaches for strength — strength in the Lord. Then the Christian can say with all his or her strength, "I put my trust in the Lord."

The circumstances in which older Christians find themselves can open them up to the varieties of prayer: internal-external, personal-group, formal-informal, ritualized-creative, spoken-sung. All varieties of prayer reinforce each other as they are appreciated and experienced. The more satisfying the varieties of prayer become, the more we realize the oneness of prayer. The result is holistic, cumulative, self-actualizing. It is life as a mature Christian.

Of the various dimensions of religious growth, those that come to the forefront at this time include:

SCRIPTURE — Time is on the side of *third age* Catholics as they approach the Bible with the leisure to read and reflect, to join study groups, to bring to bear the Word of God upon their own lifetime of experiences.

LITURGY — Celebration of the liturgy can become more than a Sunday, once-a-week experience; rather it can become involving, relaxed weekday encounters. To match the greater accessibility of the liturgy today, the *third age* Catholic can bring sensitivity, reflection and involvement.

EUCHARISTIC MINISTRY — In the special joy of bringing the Eucharist to others in the parish, *third age* Catholics give of themselves as they bring the host to shut-ins. Each Eucharistic gift that is brought becomes an exalted moment in Christian bonding.

SERVICE — In parish, neighborhood and community — as well as immediate family — there are many opportunities to use personal gifts to help others. It is Christian witness of the personal, giving kind. The more we give the more we receive — on a human as well as spiritual basis.

In the process of reaching out, inertia is a powerful

foe. The temptation to do nothing creeps in with thoughts like: "Oh, what can I do?" . . . "It doesn't really make any difference" . . . "Who needs me? There are plenty of others who can do it much better" . . . "They don't want me." . . . "So you try and try, and they don't appreciate what you're doing." . . . "No one else is doing it. Why should I?" . . . "It's enough to take care of myself without bothering about others". . . .

The opposite of inertia is reaching out. A funny thing happens. Those who do not reach out find it easy to convince themselves that there is nothing out there. Those who reach out find that there is a great deal out there. Those who care find that others care. Those who serve discover all the others who are serving. Those who love are loved.

What happens can be expressed in personal prayer that might run something like this:

> *LORD, how good and wondrous it is to identify meaning in my life by looking inward and outward. How satisfying it is to find others who are concerned about me as I become concerned about them. How uplifting to pray with others and to realize that I am part of a believing, loving group. How rewarding to look backward and see Your presence and how reassuring to look forward with confidence that Your presence will always be there. How strengthening to know that You, Lord, will fill the void and refresh those who seek after You. How wondrous to discover the peace of faith and hope, to sense the mystery of resurrection and redemption!*

TEN

Finding Fulfillment

IT IS never too late!

This basic reminder should guide older men and women toward the realization that their lives continue to unfold with opportunities to find themselves, others and the God who loves us all.

In the counter-cultural 1960s, young people reveled in the slogan, THE FUTURE IS NOW. In the 1980s, the two out five adults who are 50 or over can experience personal growth as each age of life brings its own special circumstances. Getting older is both gift and challenge. Seen in such a light, the future is not only *now*. It can be fulfilling in the active, present tense.

In the *first age* of life, as growing up and getting an education have top priority, finding oneself and gaining personal identity dominate time and energy. In the *second age*, as earning a living, building a career, and raising a family predominate, getting established and meeting responsibilities make ongoing demands in the journey forward from young adulthood. In the *third age*, as men and women reach plateaus in career and job and complete the tasks of parenting, new opportunities arise in the freedom from old responsibilities. While no one is slotted into the *third age* on a particular birthday, change in the circumstances of life is what counts. It is an age of more time and leisure and a time when the opportunities are greatest to grow in wisdom and understanding. It can be the prime of a Christian life.

Moving toward fulfillment in the *third age* of life — whether individuals are in their 50s, 60s, 70s, 80s or even 90s — begins by discarding the destructive notion of stepping aside, of disengaging from life, of putting oneself on the shelf. This is the "myth that old age is playtime and naptime, not a time to be engaged," a notion denounced by Margaret E. Kuhn, who in her 70s founded the militant Gray Panthers as an antidote to the myth. As she puts it: "The disengagement theory was postulated about 40 years ago by two white middle-aged Kansas males. They said the way in which you age successfully is to disengage yourself from what you have been doing in society all your life, and for society to disengage from you. The theory got into the thinking of millions, and it became the rationale, the philosophical basis for public policy that is age-segregated."

This mind-set is the enemy of fulfillment as men and women grow older. It points them in the direction of withdrawal instead of involvement. It encourges them to feel left out and others to leave them out. It tells people to stop living and get ready for dying. It announces that the best is over and what is coming will be worse and worse.

There are two powerful reasons for rejecting this notion:

1. It is a self-fulfilling prophecy that takes away freedom.

2. It isn't true, as *third age* men and women are demonstrating at every age through their 90s.

Other undermining attitudes follow in the wake of the disengagement myth. Men and women are tempted by the notion that getting older and becoming less active go hand in hand. They are invited to stand aside and become bystanders, to look upon their lives as a future of more or less the same (mainly less), to feel less free, more dependent. Change and danger are transformed into synonyms.

In particular, there is an insidious prejudice against older Americans — in popular attitudes, in the media, in major social and governmental institutions. Churches themselves are as likely to fall into the disengagement trap as they focus upon the problems of growing older instead of the opportunities.

As Alexander Comfort has stated in his bold and informed commentary on how America treats its older citizens: "Most of our institutions are unwittingly geared to age prejudice as in past times they were geared to race prejudice and sex prejudice. In determining needs and abilities age is quite as irrelevant as is race." (Dr. Comfort is a noted physician, physiologist, author and gerontologist.)

The message needs to be heard by everyone, but particularly by older Americans. Ironically, the very people in the midst of the demographic revolution in America are slow to understand what is happening to them. As part of an entirely new phenomenon in the history of the United States or, for that matter, the world, men and women over 50 are living healthier and more active lives than seemed possible only a few years ago. The exceptions of the past among older Americans have become the rule.

Consciousness-raising is necessary in order to add awareness to reality. Only as groups of people who are victimized grasp what is happening can they resist individually and in group action. *Third age* men and women must become aware of the prejudice of ageism, learn to reject it, and live determined to overcome it. It is not necessary to join a militant group — though many will choose to do so — but it is necessary to reject ageism consciously. Whether it has been blacks or women or any oppressed group, consciousness must change before change can be conscious.

On an individual basis, fulfillment must go beyond rejection of ageism, stereotypes and prejudice. It is necessary to become actively involved in a personal effort toward fulfillment. Three dimensions are involved:

1. Personal assessment.
2. Exploration of opportunities.
3. Action of one kind or another.

In strict logic, these would follow in a 1-2-3 sequence, but of course, life is not lived that way. All three may take place at the same time or one at a time or in any sequence. What characterizes the process is an active, self-propelling, conscious approach toward living fully in the *third age*.

Personal assessment, a form of introspection, aims at figuring out what we need, want and would like to do. It comes down to the three classic questions posed by the philosopher Kant: WHAT CAN I KNOW? WHAT OUGHT I TO DO? WHAT MAY I HOPE FOR?

In personal ways, men and women need to ask themselves what they think the world is like and what it isn't like; what the world should be, and what place do they want to have in it. More specifically, self-assessment faces questions like:

How important is where I live? What is the effect of the place where I now live?

How big a role do money and "things" play in my life?

How important is it to stay busy? What are the ways of keeping busy and working that satisfy me most?

How important is family to me? Personal relationships? Friends?

How important are routine and structure to me?

How important are adventure and risk-taking?

What things have I enjoyed doing most in the past? What does this tell me about what I can enjoy in the present and future?

For *third age* men and women who are married, these questions must not only be faced on a personal basis, but also shared with a spouse. It is unrealistic to expect a perfect match or even agreement on all major points, but sharing paves the way for mutual adjustment and accommodation.

Something vital will emerge from reflection and reassessment: personal growth. Men and women learn about themselves, feel in greater control of their selves and their lives and set the stage for greater fulfillment. The sense of discovery and of rediscovery provides a healthy tonic for living and for loving. Pleasant shocks of recognition stimulate men and women: finding new things about themselves excites them.

The late Rabbi Abraham Heschel of Jewish Theological Seminary used the phrase "formative years" to describe this process in the later years of life. He called it a time "rich in possibilities to unlearn the follies of a lifetime, to see through inbred self-deceptions, to deepen understanding and compassion."

To breathe life into answers to personal probes, men and women must seek out opportunities to follow through on what they discover or rediscover about themselves. In parish, neighborhood and community they must search for ways to fulfill their needs. There is no mystery about this. It starts with asking questions of friends, neighbors and relatives. It involves talking to church and civic organizations, watching for articles in local newspapers, noticing what others are doing. It is a matter of listening, of looking-out, of watching-out.

Taking action and following up on opportunities usually means overcoming inertia, the inclination to keep living the same old way. This is not a call to revolution and upheaval in a familiar way of life; instead it is a reminder that life is always changing and that change cannot be avoided. Openness to change and readiness to accept change is a healthy rule for living.

In a remarkable example of self-discovery, the humanist-psychologist Carl Rogers asked himself, "What is it like to be 75 years old?" He called his reflections "Growing Old: Or Older and Growing." He found himself "more open to new ideas," adding: "I feel as though a whole new depth of capacity for intimacy has been discovered in me." He immediately added with candor: "This capacity has brought me much hurt, but an even greater share of joy." (Carl R. Rogers, *A Way of Being*, Houghton Mifflin Company, Boston, 1980, p. 84.)

Across the Atlantic, another voice echoed the sense of rediscovering life at, coincidentally, the age of 75. Here is the voice of Maurice Goudeket, the devoted husband of the French writer Colette. He called his reflections *The Delights of Growing Old*:

> For my own part, when the figure 75 happens to force itself upon my attention, my first reaction is astonishment. How can I possibly have got so far? Have I not made some mistake in my reckoning? . . . .after all, it is something of a feat to have lived seventy-five years, in spite of illnesses, germs, accidents, disasters, and wars. And now every fresh day finds me more filled with wonder and better qualified to draw the last drop of delight from it. For up until now I had never known time's inexpressible wealth; and my youth had never entirely yielded itself to happiness. It is indeed this that they call growing old, this continual surge of

> memories that comes breaking in on my inner silence, this contained and sober joy, this lighthearted music that bears me up, this wider window on the world, this spreading kindly feeling and this gentleness? (Maurice Goudeket, *The Delights of Growing Old*, Farrar, Straus and Giroux, New York, 1966, pp. 4-5.)

Of course, no matter how positive and enthusiastic we are in responding to life, stress and strain are unavoidable. As the mystical poet William Blake reminds us:

> Man was made for Joy & Woe
> And when this we rightly know
> Thro the World we safely go.

The *third age*, as any age of life, makes demands, brings problems and creates anxieties. Each individual needs to develop a workable philosophy for dealing with stress. The "prescription for enjoying a full life" offered by the pathfinding biologist Hans Selye is difficult to surpass for its conciseness and validity:

• Avoid pursuit of hopeless relationships with others: "don't waste your time trying to befriend a mad dog."
• Strive with high standards, but don't be an impossible perfectionist.
• Simplify your lifestyle.
• Fight only for what is "really worth fighting for."
• Accent the positive in your life instead of the negative, focus on the pleasant aspects of life and on actions which can make life better.
• Take stock of past achievements and reflect on them as an antidote to feeling "down."
• Don't procrastinate when facing unpleasant tasks.
• Follow leaders worth following, those who deserve love, respect and gratitude.

• Remember that "no ready-made success formula" suits everybody. Work out your own formula.

The finding of personal formulas and acting on them is a lifelong process — filled with signs of life, sources of life, affirmation of life. The people who are doing this do not wear insignias. They don't need to. They are immediately recognized for what they are — men and women alive to themselves, their faith, their world and to others. They like themselves and others like them.

They have personally satisfying and fulfilling answers to questions like these:

Have I met new people that interest me?

Have I learned new things?

Have I made conscious choices? Have I decided to do something about them? Have I tried to do anything differently?

Have I taken time to be by myself and to reflect on myself, my life, my faith?

Have I had any serious conversations about myself with someone else?

Have I revealed myself and my own pain to others?

Have I tuned in on the pain and suffering of others? On their joy and celebration of life?

In terms of the Church, do I relate to it in any way differently than I did five years ago? Have I sought more from it? Have I contributed more to it?

How do I relate to the parish priest? Same, differently? How do I relate to Religious? Same, differently?

What do I expect of the parish? Have I defined the parish for myself?

How do I feel about the Church? Am I angry or satisfied with the Church? How do I feel about changes in the Church?

Have I shared these feelings with others, with the priest in a constructive way?

Do I go to confession and participate in the Eucharist in the same or different way? Do I understand and participate in the liturgy in a different way?

These personal probes aim at sensitivity, reflection and awareness. The goal is neither angry rebellion nor passive acquiescence, but fulfillment. It is a matter of taking charge of our lives as we live in the here and now.

In all this, we are not trumpeting the heroic of the unusual, but the heroics of the usual. We are talking about making a life in full awareness of the Kingdom of the Lord as manifested in the present. God did not create men and women to be bystanders in the work of creation, but participants. There is no better time for this participation than in the *third age* of life.

APPENDIX

Selected Reading

For background reading that ranges from the practical to the spiritual, here are suggestions:

Active Aging. Texts of Pope John Paul II. Vatican City: Pontifical Council for the Family, 1982.

Buckley, Joseph C. *The Retirement Handbook.* (Revised by Henry Schmidt). New York: Harper & Row, 1977.

Community Service Society of New York. *Support Groups for Caregivers of the Aged.* New York: The Natural Supports Program, 1981.

Di'Filippo and Tiso (Editors). *Aging: Spiritual Perspectives.* Lake Worth, FL: Sunday Publications, 1982.

Federal Council on Aging. *The Need for Long-Term Care: Information and Issues.* Washington, DC: U.S. Department of Health and Human Services.

Henriot, Peter and J. Holland. *Social Analysis: Linking Faith and Justice.* Second Edition. Washington, DC: Center of Concern, 1980.

Huyck, Margaret Hellie. *Growing Older: What You Need to Know About Aging.* Englewood Cliffs, NJ. Prentice Hall, 1974.

Kutza, Elizabeth A. *The Benefits of Old Age: Social-Welfare Policy for the Elderly.* Chicago: University of Chicago Press, 1980.

Levinson, Daniel J., and others. *The Seasons of a Man's Life*. Westminster, MD: Random House, 1978.

Michaels, Joseph. *The Prime of Your Life: A Practical Guide for Your Mature Years*. New York: Facts on File, 1981.

National Conference of Catholic Charities Commission on the Aging. *Serving Older Persons*. (Second Edition). Washington, DC: National Conference of Catholic Charities, 1976.

Nouwen, Henri. *The Living Reminder*. New York: Seabury, 1977.

O'Connor, Gerald. *The Second Journey: Spiritual Awareness and the Mid-Life Crisis*. New York/ Ramsey: Paulist Press, 1978.

Office for Church Life and Leadership. *The Ministry of Volunteers: A Guidebook for Churches*. New York: United Church of Christ, 1979.

Society and the Aged: Toward Reconciliation. Statement of the Catholic Bishops of the United States. Washington, DC: United States Catholic Conference Office of Publishing and Promotion Services, 1976.

State University of New York at Albany. *Basic Adult Services: A Model Curriculum*. Albany: Continuing Education Program, School of Social Welfare, 1981.

Teff, Stephanie K. *Organizing for Aging with Parish Social Ministry*. Washington, DC: National Conference of Catholic Charities, 1982.

U.S. Congress. House Select Committee on Aging. *Every Ninth American*. 97th Congress, 2nd Session. Washington, DC: 1982.

Uris, Auren. *Over 50: The Definitive Guide to Retirement*. New York: Chilton Books, 1979; Paperback, Bantam Books 1981.

Vladeck, Bruce C. *Unloving Care: The Nursing Home Tragedy.* New York: Basic Books, 1980.

Audiovisual Materials

The following audiovisual materials are available for group usage. Readers are asked to query resource for price lists and rental fees.

A Gift of Love: Remembering the Old Anew. Color filmstrip/ cassette or record; A *Gift of Love* paperback, script/ guide. Twenty-Third Publications (P.O. Box 180, West Mystic, Connecticut 06388). Created and narrated by poet, priest and photographer, Father Patrick Mooney. A reflection upon his own aging father; universal appeal. Additional copies of paperback (text of filmstrip with photos) available.

Because Somebody Cares. 27 min., 16mm, color. Northwest Cultural Films. Also available in 3/4 inch videocassette. An award winning film on how lives are enriched when young and old form friendships with each other. Helpful in recruiting volunteers.

Also available from Filmakers Library (133 East 58th St., Suite 703A, New York, New York 10022).

Luther Metke at 94. 27 min., 16mm, color. Northwest Cultural Films. Award winning documentary of a man at peace with himself and actively involved with the world around him.

Peege. 28 min., 16mm, and videocassette, color. Phoenix Films (470 Park Ave. South, New York, New York 10016). Visiting their rapidly-failing grandmother, Peege, in a nursing home at Christmas, family members engage in embarrassed, meaningless conversation. One grown grandson remembers times long ago when he and Peege spent happy times together. He finally tells Peege about his memories and that he thinks about her, prays for her and loves her. Winner of an Oscar award, this is an especially touching story.

Resource Organizations

☐ The Third Age Center, Fordham University, 113 W. 60th St. New York, NY 10023. 212-841-5347.

☐ The Center for the Study of Pre-Retirement and Aging, The Catholic University of America, Washington, DC 20064. 202-635-5483 or 5491.

☐ National Conference of Catholic Charities, 1346 Connecticut Ave., N.W., Washington, DC 20036. 202-785-2757.

☐ The Catholic Health Association, 4455 Woodson Rd., St. Louis, MO 63134. 314-427-2500.

☐ The American Association of Retired Persons, 1909 K St., N.W., Washington, DC 20049. 202-872-4700.

☐ National Society for Shut-Ins, P.O. Box 1392, Reading PA 19603. 215-374-2930.

Information on government-sponsored programs (such as Foster Grandparents, Senior Companion Program, Retired Senior Volunteer Program) can be obtained locally from the office of the county executive and from city and town halls.

Social Security Information

The Social Security Administration has a form for requesting the amount of money you have contributed: SSA-7004 PCOPI. You report your name, Social Security number, date of birth, address, any other Social Security number you have used or any other name (such as maiden name) that you have used.

The form is then signed and sent to the Social Security Administration, Wilkes-Barre Data Operations Center, P.O. Box 20, Wilkes-Barre, PA 18703.

In lieu of the form, the information can be sent in a letter.

‡ ‡ ‡